P9-DME-229

THE FAMILY Handyman

Best Organizing Solutions

CUT CLUTTER, STORE MORE, AND GAIN CLOSET SPACE

Reader's Digest

The Reader's Digest Association, Inc.
New York, NY/Montreal

A READER'S DIGEST BOOK

Copyright © 2010 The Reader's Digest Association, Inc.

All rights reserved. Unauthorized reproduction, in any manner, is prohibited.

Reader's Digest is a registered trademark of The Reader's Digest Association, Inc.

The Family Handyman is a registered trademark of RD Publications, Inc.

FOR THE FAMILY HANDYMAN
Editor in Chief: Ken Collier
Project Editor: Mary Flanagan
Senior Editors: Travis Larson, Gary Wentz
Associate Editors: Elisa Bernick, Jeff Gorton, Brett Martin
Design Director: Sara Koehler
Administrative Manager: Alice Garrett
Senior Copy Editor: Donna Bierbach
Page Layout: Teresa Marrone
Production Manager: Judy Rodriguez
Vice President, Publisher: Lora Gier
Associate Publisher, Sales: Chris Dolan

Editorial and Production Team: Steven Charbonneau, Roxie Filipkowski,
Rick Muscoplat, Mary Schwender, Bob Ungar, Bruce Wiebe, Marcia Roepke

Photography and Illustrations: Ron Chamberlain, Tom Fenenga, Bruce Kieffer, Mike Krivit,
Don Mannes, Ramon Moreno, Shawn Nielsen, Doug Oudekerk, Frank Rohrbach III, Eugene Thompson, Bill Zuehlke

FOR READER'S DIGEST
U.S. Project Editor: Kim Casey
Project Production Coordinator: Wayne Morrison
Senior Art Director: George McKeon
Executive Editor, Trade Publishing: Dolores York
Manufacturing Manager: Elizabeth Dinda
Associate Publisher, Trade Publishing: Rosanne McManus
President and Publisher, Trade Publishing: Harold Clarke

Library of Congress Cataloging-in-Publication Data
Family handyman's best organizing solutions :
cut clutter, store more, and gain closet space / from the editors of Family handyman.
    p. cm.
  ISBN 978-1-60652-170-0
1. Storage in the home. 2. Built-in furniture I. Family handyman.
  TX309.F324 2010
  648'.8--dc22

2010008837

Text, photography, and illustrations are based on articles previously run in
The Family Handyman, 2915 Commers Dr., Suite 700, Eagan, MN 55121.

We are committed to both the quality of our products and the service we provide to our customers.
We value your comments, so please feel free to contact us.

The Reader's Digest Association, Inc.
Adult Trade Publishing
44 S. Broadway
White Plains, NY 10601

For more Reader's Digest products and information, visit our website:
www.rd.com (in the United States)
For more information about *The Family Handyman* magazine, visit
www.thefamilyhandyman.com.

Printed in China

7 9 10 8 6

WARNING

All do-it-yourself activities involve a degree of risk. Skills,
materials, tools, and site conditions vary widely. Although
the editors have made every effort to ensure accuracy, the reader
remains responsible for the selection and use of tools, materials,
and methods. Always obey local codes and laws, follow
manufacturer's operating instructions, and observe safety precautions.

Contents

1 Organize your
garage

The garage tends to be a dumping ground for everything from lawn chairs to sports gear and oversized grocery items. When you start parking on the street because your car no longer fits, it's time to fight back! Here we've gathered our best storage tricks and tips, plus ideas for space-saving overhead storage and a nifty cabinet for car-care tools and supplies.

And don't miss the special section on storing sports gear on page 20.

Overhead storage

Look up! Unused storage space is right over your head.

BEND HOOKS
IN VISE TO
FIT ON PIPE

1/2" PIPE

1/2" FLOOR
FLANGE

3" x 1/2"
NIPPLE

1/2" 90°
FITTING

3" S-HOOK

Sturdy cord and tool hanger

Store a load of cords, air hoses, ropes and tools on this rugged rack. To build one, you'll need:

- One 3- or 4-ft. x 1/2-in. iron pipe threaded on both ends
- Two 3-in. x 1/2-in. pipe nipples
- Two 1/2-in. 90-degree pipe fittings
- Two 1/2-in. floor flanges
- Several 3-in. S-hooks
- Cable Clamps ($25 for a 13-pack of medium-size clamps at cableclamp.com, 727-528-1000, or look for them at home centers). Also you can use leftover strips of plastic-sheathed electrical cable.

Assemble the pipe, elbows, nipples and floor flanges, then screw through the flanges to a horizontal 2x4 set at shoulder height on a shop wall. Attach your S-hooks. If yours don't fit, clamp the hooks in a vise and bend open one end just enough to fit on the pipe after assembly. Now snap Cable Clamps on all your coils and hang them from the S-hooks.

CABLE CLAMPS

Upside-down shelves!

Here's some neat and fast storage for your shop's upper regions. Bolt together a set of inexpensive metal shelves (about $12 at a home center) and attach them upside down to the ceiling joists with lag bolts. The spacing between shelves is completely adjustable. Hang the shelves so they're easy to reach, or set them high so you won't bonk your head. Trim the shelf posts to just the right height with tin snips.

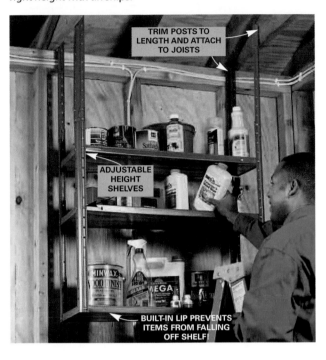

TRIM POSTS TO LENGTH AND ATTACH TO JOISTS

ADJUSTABLE HEIGHT SHELVES

BUILT-IN LIP PREVENTS ITEMS FROM FALLING OFF SHELF!

Double-duty shelf brackets

Shelf brackets designed to support clothes hanger rods aren't just for closets. The rod-holding hook on these brackets comes in handy in the garage and workshop too. You can bend the hook to suit long tools or cords. Closet brackets cost about $3 each at home centers and hardware stores.

Hang-it-all hooks

Those plastic hooks that plumbers use to support pipes make convenient hangers for just about anything. They're strong, cheap (25¢ to $1 each) and come in a range of sizes. Find them in the plumbing aisle at home centers and hardware stores.

Simple storage rack

Use this storage rack for lumber and other long stuff. Simply drill a line of 3/4-in. holes about 1 1/2 in. deep in adjacent studs, angling the holes slightly downward. Then insert 15-in.-long sections of 1/2-in. galvanized pipe. Keep the lowest pipes at least 6 ft. above the floor so you won't crack your skull on them.

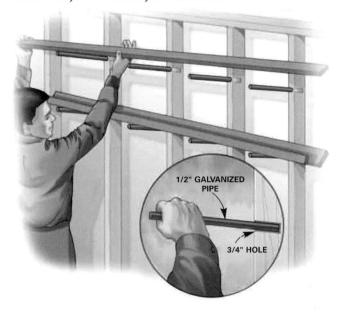

1/2" GALVANIZED PIPE

3/4" HOLE

Suspended shelving

Make good use of the space above your garage doors

Tuck medium and lightweight stuff onto shelves suspended from the ceiling. The shelves are designed to fit into that unused space above the garage doors (you need 16 in. of clearance to fit a shelf and standard 12-1/2-in.-high plastic bins). However, you can adjust the shelf height and put them anywhere. The only limitation is weight. This 4 x 6-ft. shelf is designed to hold about 160 lbs., a load that typical ceiling framing can safely support. It's best to save the shelf for "deep storage," using labeled bins with lids, because you'll need a stepladder to reach the contents of the bins.

First find which way the trusses run, then hang one shelf support from three adjacent trusses (Photo 2). The trusses above are 24 in. apart; if yours are spaced at 16 in., skip one intermediate truss. These shelves were built to hold bins, but if you put loose stuff up there, add 1x4 sides to keep things from falling.

Assemble the 2x4s as shown (Figure A), using 5-in. corner braces (1-in. x 5-in. Stanley corner brace, $2.84 at home centers) and 1/4-in. x 1-in. hex head lag screws (drill pilot holes first).

Now attach the corner braces on both ends of a shelf support to the center of a truss by drilling pilot holes and using 1/4-in. x 2-in. hex head lag screws (Photo 2). The only challenge is finding the center of trusses through a drywall ceiling (if your ceiling is finished) to attach the shelf supports. Tap a small nail through the drywall until you locate both edges of the truss. Measure to find the center of the adjacent trusses, and measure to keep the three supports in alignment with one another. Finish the shelf unit by attaching a 3/8-in. x 4-ft. x 6-ft. plywood floor (Photo 3).

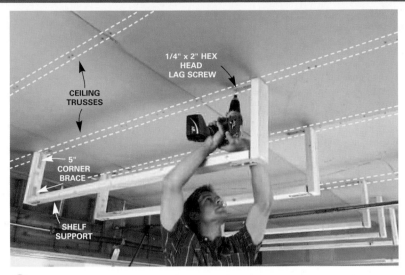

NEED 16" MINIMUM

1 Measure from the ceiling to the top of the raised garage door. Subtract 1 in. to determine the height of the side 2x4s.

1/4" x 2" HEX HEAD LAG SCREW

CEILING TRUSSES

5" CORNER BRACE

SHELF SUPPORT

2 Build three identical shelf supports, align the side supports, and predrill and lag-screw each into the center of the ceiling trusses.

3/8" PLYWOOD BASE

3 Cut 3/8-in. plywood for the shelf base and attach it to the 2x4 shelf supports with 1-in. wood screws.

4 Don't overload bins with heavy stuff. Limit the total weight to about 160 lbs.

One shelf holds all this!

Each shelf holds eight containers 16 in. wide x 24 in. long x 12-1/2 in. high.

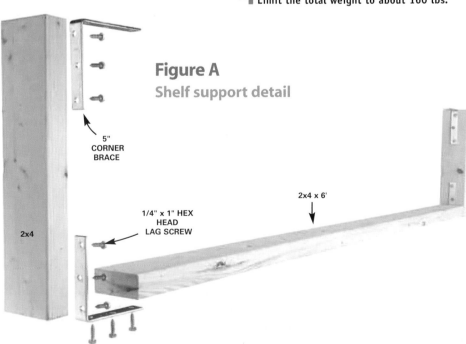

Figure A
Shelf support detail

5" CORNER BRACE

2x4

1/4" x 1" HEX HEAD LAG SCREW

2x4 x 6'

Easy lawn chair storage

Here's how to store your lawn and folding chairs so they're out of your way. Take two pieces of 1x4 lumber (any scrap lumber will do) and create some simple, cheap and useful brackets on the wall. Cut each board 7-3/4 in. long with a 30-degree angle on both ends. Fasten pairs of these brackets with three 2-in. screws to the side of the exposed wall studs, directly across from each other, and you've got a perfect place to hang your chairs.

Garage ceiling track storage

If you store stuff in big plastic storage bins and you need a place to put them, how about the garage ceiling? Screw 2x2s to the ceiling framing with 3-1/2-in. screws spaced every 2 ft. Use the bins as a guide for spacing the 2x2s. The lips on the bins should just brush against the 2x2s when you're sliding the bins into place. Then center and screw 1x4s to the 2x2s with 2-in. screws. The garage ceiling is a perfect place to store light and medium-weight seasonal items like holiday decorations and camping gear.

Up-and-away storage

The perfect place to store small quantities of long, narrow offcuts and moldings is right over your head. Build this set of overhead storage racks either in high basement ceilings or in the open trusses in garage shops. Use 2x6s for the vertical hangers and doubled-up 3/4-in. plywood for the lower angled supports. Secure each 2x6 into the framing with two 5/16 x 3-in. lag screws. Screw each hanger into the 2x6 with two offset 5/16 x 3-in. lags. The angle on the supports keeps stuff from sliding off.

Car care cabinet

Simple shelves, plus a handy worktable

It's a whole lot easier to be a gearhead when all your gear is in one place. Here's an easy-to-build organizer you can complete in one morning, even if you're a beginning DIYer. If you build it from construction-grade pine boards and plywood, the materials will cost you about $40. If you use maple boards and birch plywood as shown here, it will cost about $70. The only must-have power tools for this project are a drill and a circular saw, although a table saw and a miter saw make the job much faster and easier.

To get started, cut the sides to length, lay them back to back and mark the shelf locations (Photo 1). Then mark and drill 3/16-in. pilot holes for the screws that fasten the shelves. Measure 1 in. and 2-3/4 in. from the back edges of the sides when you locate these holes. Set the 1x4 shelves between the sides and drill pilot holes into the shelf ends using the holes in the sides as guides. Drilling these pilot holes and screwing the shelves into place is easier if you clamp the whole cabinet together first (Photo 2). But you can hand-hold the shelves against the sides if you don't have long clamps. After the shelves are screwed into place, rip 1/4-in. plywood into

Figure A
Car care cabinet

Overall dimensions: 34" tall x 24" wide x 5-3/4" deep

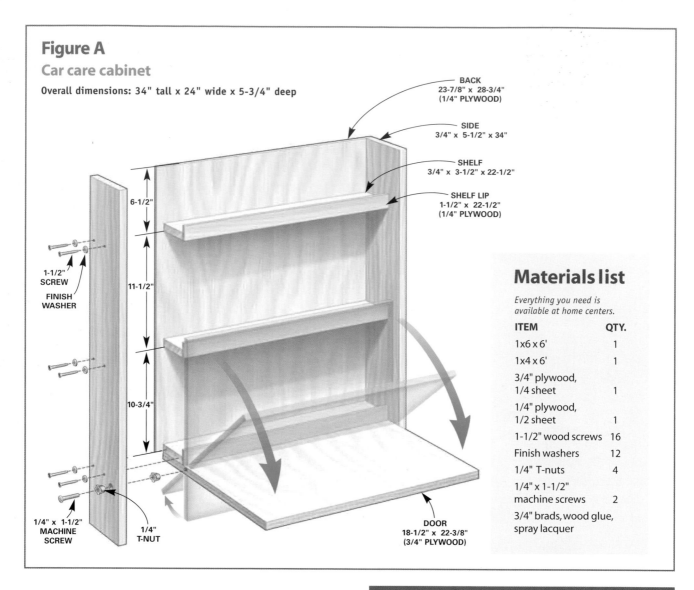

BACK
23-7/8" x 28-3/4"
(1/4" PLYWOOD)

SIDE
3/4" x 5-1/2" x 34"

SHELF
3/4" x 3-1/2" x 22-1/2"

SHELF LIP
1-1/2" x 22-1/2"
(1/4" PLYWOOD)

6-1/2"

11-1/2"

10-3/4"

1-1/2"
SCREW

FINISH
WASHER

1/4" x 1-1/2"
MACHINE
SCREW

1/4"
T-NUT

DOOR
18-1/2" x 22-3/8"
(3/4" PLYWOOD)

Materials list

Everything you need is available at home centers.

ITEM	QTY.
1x6 x 6'	1
1x4 x 6'	1
3/4" plywood, 1/4 sheet	1
1/4" plywood, 1/2 sheet	1
1-1/2" wood screws	16
Finish washers	12
1/4" T-nuts	4
1/4" x 1-1/2" machine screws	2
3/4" brads, wood glue, spray lacquer	

1-1/2-in.-wide strips for the front lips on the shelves. Glue the lips to the shelves, using 3/4-in. brads or clamps to hold the lips in place while the glue sets.

To complete the cabinet box, lay it face down and make sure it's square by taking diagonal measurements. Then run light beads of wood glue on the sides and shelves and tack on the plywood back with 3/4-in. brads spaced about 8 in. apart. The back is slightly narrower than the cabinet, so you don't have to line up the edges perfectly.

Flip the cabinet onto its back and clamp the door into place with the back edge of the door resting flat on your workbench. Using a square, mark the location of the door on the outer sides of the cabinet. Then drill 5/16-in. holes 1-3/8 in. from the front edges of the cabinet sides. Drill through the sides and into the door, stopping at a depth of about 1-1/2 in. (Photo 3). Cut shallow recesses in the door for the T-nuts using a coarse file or wood rasp. Position the door and drive in the machine screws that act as pivot points for the door. Make sure the door opens and closes freely. If not, sand down the edges that bind with a belt sander or an orbital sander. If the fit is a bit sloppy, remove one of the screws and place a washer over the T-nut.

A fold-up door

The worktable is also a door that encloses the bottom shelf. Flip it up and you've got a mounting surface for a towel holder and other accessories. You can mount a fold-up door on special hinges, but a faster method that requires just a couple of bucks' worth of hardware is shown in Photos 3 and 4.

1 Prevent mistakes by marking shelf locations on both cabinet sides at once. Then mark the screw locations and drill pilot holes.

2 Clamp the shelves between the sides and screw the cabinet together. Give the exposed screw heads a neater look with finish washers.

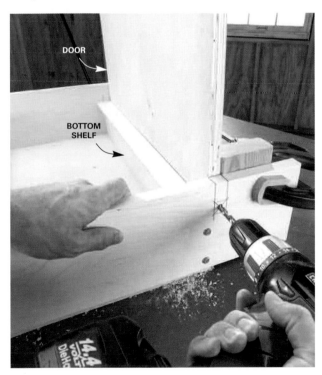

3 Drill the T-nut holes with the door locked tight against the bottom shelf. Drill as straight as you can through the sides and into the door.

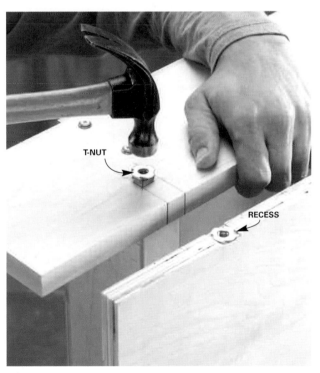

4 Drive the T-nuts into the holes. File the recesses so the T-nuts sit flush with the edges of the door. Attach the door with machine screws.

To put a quick finish on the cabinet, remove the door. Sand away any pencil marks and smooth sharp edges. Take the cabinet to a well-ventilated area and apply a couple of light coats of aerosol spray lacquer. The lacquer will harden in just a few minutes. Then lightly sand with a fine sand-ing sponge and spray on a final coat. Wait about an hour to reattach the door. To mount the cabinet, drive four 1-1/2-in. screws through the back and into studs. Add a dry-erase board and paper towel holder if you like, and load those shelves!

Tips for a tidy garage

WOOD BLOCK

Save your lawn products

Leave a bag of fertilizer or weed killer open for long and it'll soak up moisture from the air and won't go through a spreader. Even grass seed could use an extra layer of protection from a moisture-wicking concrete floor. Place opened bags of lawn products in large resealable plastic bags ($1 at discount stores). The products will be free of clumps or pests when you need them.

GIANT RESEALABLE
PLASTIC BAG

Storage tubes

Cardboard concrete-forming tubes are inexpensive ($7 at any home center) and provide a great place to store baseball bats, long-handled tools and rolls of just about anything. Rest the tubes on a piece of 2x4 to keep them high and dry. Secure each tube to a garage stud with a plumbing strap.

WOOD
BLOCK

Dustpan caddy

Keep a dustpan handy with an "unbreakable" wall file holder ($8) from an office-supply store. Attach the file holder to the garbage can with 8-32 x 3/4-in. machine bolts and nuts. Position the screw heads inside the garbage can so the bag doesn't snag on the end of the bolt.

More projects online

If you're looking for more garage storage projects, visit thefamilyhandyman.com and search for "garage storage." You'll find the pegboard bin, plywood rack and shovel rack shown here. There's also a pegboard cabinet, multipurpose towers, rotating corner shelves, and five different workbenches.

Suspended extension ladder

It's always most convenient to hang an extension ladder on brackets on a wall. But unfortunately that wipes out all other storage potential for that wall. To save that valuable wall space, here's a pair of 2x4 suspended brackets so a ladder can be stored flat along the ceiling.

Simply slide one end of the ladder into one bracket, then lift and slide the other end into the other bracket. Most people will need to stand on something solid to reach the second bracket. The 2x4 bracket sides are 16 in. long with 5-in. corner braces lag-screwed into the top for attachment to the ceiling truss (Figure A).

The bracket base is a 1/2-in. x 24-in. threaded steel rod ($2.75) that extends through 5/8-in. drilled holes on the bracket sides. It's held in place with flat/lock washers and a nut on each side of both 2x4 uprights. A 3/4-in. x 18-in.-long piece of PVC conduit pipe surrounds the rod for smooth rolling action when you slide the ladder in and out.

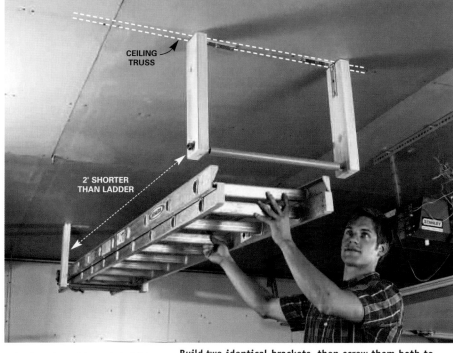

Build two identical brackets, then screw them both to ceiling trusses with 1/4 x 2-in. lag screws. Space the brackets so the ladder will extend at least 1 ft. beyond the end of each one.

> **CAUTION**
> For extra security, wrap a bungee cord around the ladder and one bracket.

Figure A Ladder support detail

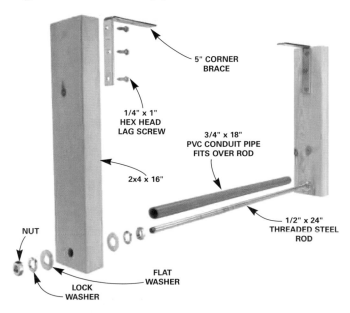

5" CORNER BRACE

1/4" x 1" HEX HEAD LAG SCREW

3/4" x 18" PVC CONDUIT PIPE FITS OVER ROD

2x4 x 16"

1/2" x 24" THREADED STEEL ROD

NUT

FLAT WASHER

LOCK WASHER

Lawn chair brackets

Don't throw away those old lawn chairs. Cut out all the right angles of the frames and use them as hanging brackets. The reinforced corners are surprisingly strong. Just drill holes for screws, then squeeze closed the ends of the horizontal sections in a vise. Bend these ends up about 1 in. to keep things from falling off the brackets.

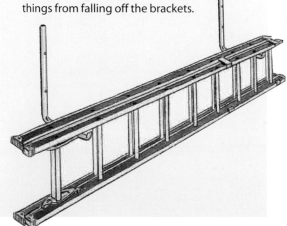

Garage storage center

Five easy options for five kinds of garage clutter

If you have an attached garage, the door to the house is probably a dumping ground for shoes, sports gear, jackets and all kinds of other stuff that you don't have space for indoors. These five cabinets can eliminate that mess so you don't have to walk through an obstacle course to get in the house. Each cabinet is a simple box that has been customized to solve a different storage problem. Build one or all five.

You can build, install and load these cabinets in a weekend. The only power tools you'll need are a drill and a circular saw.

But a table saw and a sliding miter saw are handy for ripping and crosscutting the plywood, and a brad nailer helps tack the cabinets and drawers together before you drive the screws.

Each cabinet requires one sheet of plywood or less and costs about $50, including the hardware and finish. The project shown is birch plywood ($40 per sheet). You could use oak plywood ($48) or even MDF ($30). For the pantry cabinet you'll need 1/4-in. plywood for the drawer bottoms. All the materials are available at home centers except the drawer slides for the pantry cabinet.

Box assembly tips

These cabinets are surprisingly easy to build. The illustrations tell you most of what you need to know. Here are some tips for smooth assembly:

- If you don't have a table saw to rip the plywood, use a saw guide and a circular saw (Photo 1).
- Use a shorter saw guide or a sliding miter saw to get straight, square crosscuts.
- Drill 1/8-in. pilot holes to prevent splitting. Keep screws 1 in. from edges.
- If you have a brad nailer, tack parts together to make drilling easier. But don't rely on brads alone—you still need screws. If you don't have a brad nailer, use clamps (Photo 2).
- If your cuts were slightly off and the top, bottom and sides aren't exactly the same width, don't worry. Just make sure the front edges of the box are flush.
- Attach the screw strip to the top before attaching the side pieces.
- Attach hardware (drawer slides, shelf standards) to the sides before building the box.
- Screw the top, bottom and any fixed shelves onto one side before attaching the other side.

SAW GUIDE

1 Get perfectly straight, accurate cuts with a circular saw using a homemade saw guide. Clamp the saw guide at your mark on the plywood.

SCREW STRIP

2 Clamp the frame parts together, including the screw strip. Drill pilot holes and drive screws.

$50 and 3 hours per cabinet

These cabinets were designed with economy and speed in mind. Here are three tricks to cut costs and assembly time:

- Size all parts to use the plywood efficiently. The sides, for example, are just under 12 in. wide (11-7/8 in.), so you'll get four from a 4 x 8-ft. sheet.
- Eliminate the cabinet backs, saving time and materials. Just be sure to handle the cabinets gently—they're a bit flimsy until they're screwed to the wall.
- Apply the finish before assembly. After you cut the parts to size, sand everything with 120-grit sandpaper and apply a coat of Minwax Wipe-On Poly ($9 per pint).

STUD LOCATIONS

CLEAT

3 Set the cabinets on a cleat, then screw them to the wall at the studs (use tape to mark the stud locations). Drive screws through the cabinet bottoms into the cleat.

Wet clothes cabinet

An airy hangout for damp or dirty coats and boots

The wire shelves in this cabinet allow boots to drip dry and air to circulate freely so clothes will dry. The extra-wide screw strip lets you attach coat hooks. To build the cabinet, you'll need 6 ft. of 12-in.-deep wire shelving ($6) and coat hooks (starting at $2.60 each).

Attach the back cleats flush with the sides. Inset the front cleats 1/4 in. Cut the wire shelves at 22-1/4 in. This gives you 1/8 in. of play on each side. Cut the shelves with bolt cutters or have the home center cut them for you. The metal in the shelves is very tough and hard to cut with a hacksaw.

Place plastic end caps ($1.30 for a pack of 14) over the shelf ends. Secure the shelves to the front cleats with C-clamps ($5.70 for a pack of 20). Fasten two clamps per shelf. Hold the coat hooks in place in the cabinet, drill pilot holes and then drive the screws that came with the hooks to fasten them in place.

SCREW STRIP
3/4" x 10" x 22-1/2"

SIDES
3/4" x 11-7/8" x 72"

WIRE SHELVES
12" x 22-1/4"

C-CLAMP

CLEATS
3/4" x 2" x 22-1/2"

1/4" INSET

Open shelf cabinet

Spacious, adjustable shelves that cut garage clutter

This open-shelf cabinet needs a fixed shelf in the middle to keep the sides from bowing, but you can make the rest of the shelves adjustable. Install as many adjustable shelves as you want—this cabinet can hold a lot of stuff!

You'll need four 6-ft. shelf standards ($3.30 each) for this cabinet. Get started by marking the shelf standard locations and the fixed middle shelf location on the two cabinet sides. Cut the shelf standards to length with a hacksaw, then screw them to the sides above and below the fixed shelf marks.

Install the adjustable shelves after you hang the cabinet on the wall.

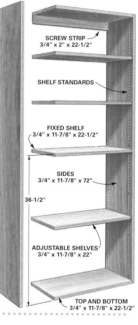

SCREW STRIP
3/4" x 2" x 22-1/2"

SHELF STANDARDS

FIXED SHELF
3/4" x 11-7/8" x 22-1/2"

SIDES
3/4" x 11-7/8" x 72"

36-1/2"

ADJUSTABLE SHELVES
3/4" x 11-7/8" x 22"

TOP AND BOTTOM
3/4" x 11-7/8" x 22-1/2"

Sports gear cabinet

A compact organizer for all kinds of equipment

The cabinet dividers let you store long-handled sports gear, like hockey sticks, bats and rackets. The lip on the top shelf keeps balls from falling off. Nail the lip to the shelf before installing the shelf at any height that suits your needs.

When installing the dividers, cut two 7-in. spacers and place them between the cabinet sides and the dividers to keep the dividers straight as you install the cabinet face.

Measure diagonally from box corner to corner to make sure the cabinet is square before attaching the face. Set the face on the cabinet, leaving a 1/8-in. reveal along both sides and the bottom. Drill pilot holes and screw the face to the sides and the dividers.

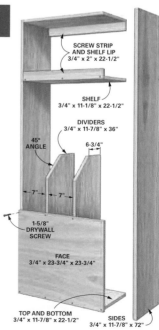

SCREW STRIP
AND SHELF LIP
3/4" x 2" x 22-1/2"

SHELF
3/4" x 11-1/8" x 22-1/2"

DIVIDERS
3/4" x 11-7/8" x 36"

45° ANGLE

6-3/4"

7"   7"

1-5/8"
DRYWALL
SCREW

FACE
3/4" x 23-3/4" x 23-3/4"

TOP AND BOTTOM
3/4" x 11-7/8" x 22-1/2"

SIDES
3/4" x 11-7/8" x 72"

Shoe and boot cabinet

Eliminate the footwear pileup on the back steps

The lower shelves in this cabinet hold boots and shoes, while the cubbyholes at the top are for slippers and sandals. The screw strip is lower in this cabinet than it is in the rest, but it'll still hold the cabinet in place.

Install the lower shelf first, then add the divider and screw on the shelves that fit between the divider and the cabinet sides.

Build the cubbyholes on your work surface, then stick the assembled cubbies into the cabinet. Start by screwing two dividers onto a shelf. Make two shelves this way. Then install a center divider between these two shelves. Add a shelf to the bottom, over the two dividers. Then insert the cubbies inside the cabinet and screw through the sides into the shelves and through the top into the dividers.

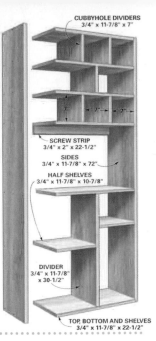

CUBBYHOLE DIVIDERS
3/4" x 11-7/8" x 7"

7"   7"   7"

SCREW STRIP
3/4" x 2" x 22-1/2"

SIDES
3/4" x 11-7/8" x 72"

HALF SHELVES
3/4" x 11-7/8" x 10-7/8"

DIVIDER
3/4" x 11-7/8"
x 30-1/2"

TOP, BOTTOM AND SHELVES
3/4" x 11-7/8" x 22-1/2"

Hanging the cabinets

Install a 2x2 cleat on the wall for the cabinets to sit on. You'll need 24 in. of cleat for each cabinet. Keep the cleat at least 8 in. above the floor so you can sweep under the cabinets.

Snap a level chalk line on the wall for the cleat (measure down from the ceiling if your floor slopes!). Attach the cleat at the chalk line by driving a 3-in. drywall screw into each stud. Set the cabinets on the cleats. Place a level alongside the cabinet to make sure it's standing plumb and square. Then drill pilot holes through the screw strips and attach the cabinets to the wall with 3-in. drywall screws. Screw adjoining cabinets together by driving 1-1/4-in. drywall screws through the side near the top and the bottom.

NOTE: All cabinets are 11-7/8" deep x 24" wide x 72" tall.

SCREW STRIP
3/4" x 2" x 22-1/2"

DOOR
3/4" x 23-3/4"
x 29-3/8"

ADJUSTABLE SHELF
3/4" x 11-7/8"
x 22"

SHELF STANDARDS

FIXED SHELF
3/4" x 11-7/8"
x 22-1/2"

SIDES
3/4" x 11-7/8"
x 72"

10" O.C.

43"

RAIL
3/4" x 2" x 22-1/2"

12" O.C.

12" O.C.

TOP AND BOTTOM
3/4" x 11-7/8" x 22-1/2"

Pantry cabinet

Bulk storage that frees up kitchen space

If you buy groceries in bulk, this is the storage solution for you. The bottom drawers in this cabinet are deep enough to hold two cases of soda. The top drawers are perfect for canned goods or bottled water. The upper shelves are adjustable for more bulk storage. The cabinet faces and door keep everything enclosed.

Inexpensive drawer slides let the drawers open and close easily. The ones shown are from Woodworker's Hardware ($4 per set of two, including screws; No. B230M 12CM; wwhardware.com). You'll also need two 6-ft. shelf standards ($3.30 for 6 ft.).

Lay the cabinet sides next to each other and mark the center for each drawer slide. Place a slide over each mark, drill pilot holes (a $7 self-centering drill bit works best) and screw the slides into place. Cut the shelf standards with a hacksaw and screw them to the cabinet sides, above the fixed shelf.

Assemble the drawers with 1-5/8-in. screws. Place the drawer slides on the drawers, drill pilot holes and attach them with screws. Test-fit them in the cabinet. If the cabinet sides are bowed even slightly, attach a 2-in. rail in the back to hold the sides in place so the drawers slide smoothly.

Fasten the faces to the drawers with 1-1/4-in. screws driven from inside the drawers. Build the handles with leftover plywood and attach them with 2-in. screws (driven from the inside).

Attach the door to the cabinet with 1/2-in. overlay hinges, also called half-wrap hinges ($1.70 each). They're available at home centers or wwhardware.com (No. A07550).

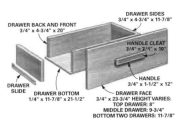

DRAWER SIDES
3/4" x 4-3/4" x 11-7/8"

DRAWER BACK AND FRONT
3/4" x 4-3/4" x 20"

HANDLE CLEAT
3/4" x 2/4" x 10"

DRAWER SLIDE

DRAWER BOTTOM
1/4" x 11-7/8" x 21-1/2"

DRAWER FACE
3/4" x 23-3/4" HEIGHT VARIES:
TOP DRAWER: 8"
MIDDLE DRAWER: 9-3/4"
BOTTOM TWO DRAWERS: 11-7/8"

HANDLE
3/4" x 1-1/2" x 12"

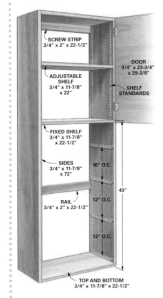

Balls, bats, bikes and more!

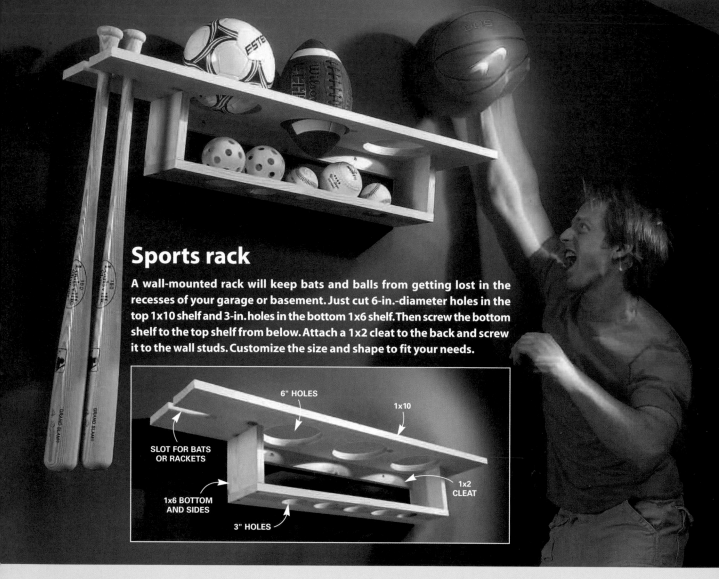

Sports rack

A wall-mounted rack will keep bats and balls from getting lost in the recesses of your garage or basement. Just cut 6-in.-diameter holes in the top 1x10 shelf and 3-in. holes in the bottom 1x6 shelf. Then screw the bottom shelf to the top shelf from below. Attach a 1x2 cleat to the back and screw it to the wall studs. Customize the size and shape to fit your needs.

6" HOLES

1x10

SLOT FOR BATS
OR RACKETS

1x6 BOTTOM
AND SIDES

3" HOLES

1x2
CLEAT

Fishing rod catcher

Cut an 8-ft. 1x4 in half and use 1-in. screws to mount 1-1/4-in. PVC caps (42¢ each) on one 1x4 4 in. apart. On the second 1x4, equally space 1-1/4-in. PVC couplings (35¢ each). Screw the 1x4 with the caps to the wall a foot off the floor, and the one with couplings 6 ft. off the floor and directly above it. The rod tips slide up through the couplings and the handles rest in the caps.

Cheap storage cylinders

Build cheap storage cylinders from PVC pipe, end caps, female adapters and cleanout plugs. Parts are available in an assortment of diameters at any hardware store or home center. Cut the pipe to length with a handsaw or chop saw. Glue an end cap to one end and a female adapter to the other pipe end with PVC cement. Twist in a threaded cleanout plug for a cap. If sealing isn't important, you can drill holes in the pipe to decrease the cylinder's weight. Use the cylinders to store and protect fishing rods, drill bits, cross-country skis, blueprints or anything long and skinny—you name it.

FEMALE ADAPTER

CLEANOUT PLUG

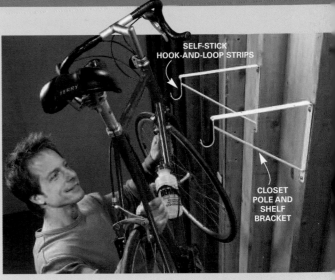

SELF-STICK HOOK-AND-LOOP STRIPS

CLOSET POLE AND SHELF BRACKET

Bike rack

Closet pole and shelf brackets can keep your bikes up and out of the way of car doors and bumpers. Just screw the brackets to the wall studs. Line the pole carriage with self-stick hook-and-loop strips so it won't scratch your bike frame.

Under-joist shelf

Create extra storage space by screwing wire closet shelving to joists in your garage or basement. Wire shelving is see-through, so you can easily tell what's up there. Depending on the width, wire shelves cost from $1 to $3 per foot at home centers.

Movable bike rack

Tired of that darn bike hanging in your way? Build this movable bike rack from a 2x4 and a pair of bicycle hooks. Cut four 3-1/2-in. blocks, stack two on top of each other, and screw them together. Now screw them on the end of a 4-ft. 2x4 and repeat the process for the other side. Drill a hole in the middle of the stacked blocks and screw in the bicycle hooks. Lay the rack across your garage ceiling trusses, and hang your bike from the hooks. When you need to get behind the bike, simply slide the entire rack out of the way.

Fishing rod holder

Here's an easy way to store fishing rods so they're out of the way. Use two pieces of 1/4-in. or thicker plywood, 8 in. wide or so. Drill holes in one piece, and slots in the other. Screw them to your garage rafters.

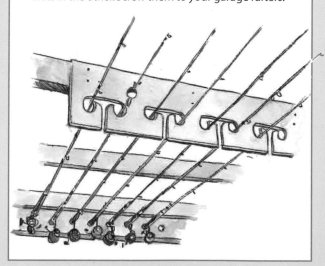

Ski and pole organizer

Keep your skis up and easy to find with this simple 2x4 rack. Drill 3/4-in.-diameter holes spaced 3/4 in. apart. Glue 4-1/2-in. lengths of 3/4-in. dowel into the holes and then mount the 2x4 to the wall studs. Space the groupings about 8 in. apart to make room for ski bindings. Now you'll spend less time looking for your skis and more time on the trails.

SCREW   DRIP TRAYS

Stay-put balls

Keep sport balls off the floor and out of the way by resting them in flowerpot drip trays (80¢ at home centers). Screw the trays down to an inexpensive shelving unit. The balls will stay put.

Organize your
kitchen & bathrooms

Some of the most public spaces in your home are the kitchen and the bathrooms. Usually these rooms lack sufficient storage space, and if something is sitting on the counter or vanity, it's out there for all to see!

Here you'll find more than 20 simple, inexpensive ways to tidy up these high-traffic rooms. Plus we've included complete instructions for building two styles of handy kitchen cabinet rollouts.

Kitchen cabinet & drawer upgrades

Cutting board rack

You can make this nifty rack for less than $10 and mount it inside a cabinet door to stash your cutting boards out of sight. It goes together in a snap since it only requires a 6-ft. 1x2 and two L-brackets.

Measure between the door stiles to get the maximum width of your rack. Make sure the rack will be wide enough for your cutting board (or spring for a new one). You'll also need to mount the rack low enough so it doesn't bump into a cabinet shelf when the door closes. Cut the bottom and face rails to match the space between the cabinet door stiles.

Cut the sides 7-1/4 in. long. Nail the sides to the base. Then nail the two face pieces at the top and bottom to complete the rack (Photo 1). The easiest way to mount the rack is to take the cabinet door off its hinges and lay it down. Predrill the screw holes for the L-brackets and mount the rack to the cabinet door using a 1-in. L-bracket centered on each side of the rack (Photo 2).

FACE RAIL

BOTTOM RAIL

1 Nail the base rail to the sides, then nail on the face rails. For a quick, clear finish, spray on two light coats of lacquer.

DOOR STILE

L-BRACKET

2 Mount the rack on the door with L-brackets. This is easiest if you remove the door. Be sure to predrill screw holes in the door stiles.

Adjustable spice shelf

This in-cabinet spice shelf puts small containers at eye level and still leaves room in the cabinet for tall items. The materials will cost you less than $10. You'll need a 4-ft. 1x3 for the top shelf and a 4-ft. 1x2 for the bottom ledger. You can find shelf pegs at home centers in two sizes, 1/4 in. and 3/16 in., so measure the holes in your cabinet before you shop. The secret is to assemble the shelf outside the cabinet and then set it on the shelf pegs.

Measure the sides and back of your cabinet and cut your shelf and ledger pieces. Subtract 1/8 in. from all sides so you can fit the unit into the cabinet. Attach the sides to the back of the bottom ledger and put two nails into each butt joint. Then nail the top shelf sides into place and pin the shelf back at the corners to hold it flush (Photo 1).

To install the shelf unit, carefully fit one end of the "U" into the cabinet, holding it higher at one end, and shimmy it down until it sits firmly on top of the shelf pegs (Photo 2). Shift the pegs up or down to adjust the shelf height. Spray a quick coat of lacquer on the shelf before installing it.

BACK SHELF

SIDE SHELF

BACK LEDGER

SIDE LEDGER

1 Nail the back and side ledgers together, then nail on the side shelves. Measure between the side shelves and cut the back shelf to fit.

SHELF PEGS

2 Set the spice shelf on adjustable shelf pegs. You may have to remove an existing shelf so you can tilt the spice shelf into place.

Blind-corner glide-out and swing-out shelves

Blind-corner cabinets—those with a blank face that allows another cabinet to butt into them—may be great for aging wine, but they're darn near impossible to see and reach into. This pair of accessories puts an end to this hidden wasteland. The hinged shelf swings out of the way, and the gliding shelf slides forward so you can access food items stored in the back. You can use the same hardware and techniques for making base cabinets more accessible too.

The key measurements and clearances:

Glide-out shelf dimensions. You can only make the unit as long as the door opening is wide (or else you can't fit it in!). Make the unit about 1/2 in. narrower than the inside width of the cabinet.

Swing-out tray dimensions. The corner-to-corner or diagonal measurement of the unit (Figure A) can't exceed the width of the door opening (or else that won't fit either!). Make the unit about 1 in. shorter than the opening height so it has room to swing freely when installed.

Piano hinges and bottom slides are available from Rockler Woodworking and Hardware, 4365 Willow Drive, Medina, MN 55340; (800) 279-4441. rockler.com. The front moldings are manufactured by House of Fara (800-334-1732; houseoffara.com). House of Fara products are available at home centers. Call the company if you need help finding a dealer.

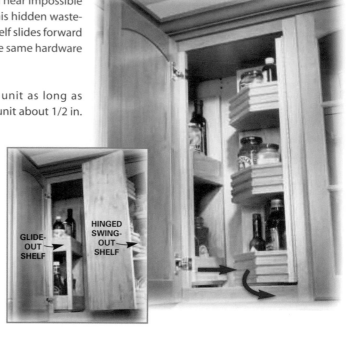

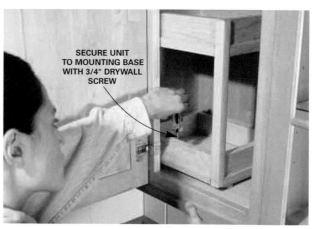

GLIDE-OUT SHELF

HINGED SWING-OUT SHELF

Build the glide-out shelf

1x3

1/2" PLYWOOD BOTTOM

3d FINISH NAILS

1 Glue and nail the 1x3s together using 4d finish nails, then secure the plywood bottom with 3d finish nails.

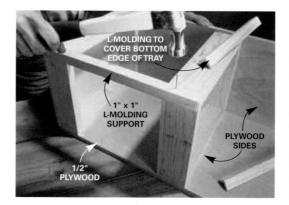

L-MOLDING TO COVER BOTTOM EDGE OF TRAY

1" x 1" L-MOLDING SUPPORT

1/2" PLYWOOD

PLYWOOD SIDES

2 Cut out the two plywood sides, then glue and nail the corners. Connect the trays to the two plywood sides using 1-in. drywall screws, then cut and nail L-molding to support the front corner. Cut and install L-moldings to support and cover the exposed plywood edges of the upper tray. Install 3/4-in. screen molding to cover the plywood edges of the bottom tray.

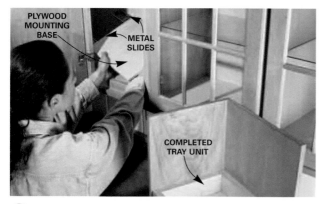

PLYWOOD MOUNTING BASE

METAL SLIDES

COMPLETED TRAY UNIT

3 Cut the mounting base plywood slightly smaller than the other tray bottoms, then secure the two slides parallel to each other about 1 in. from each edge. Slip this mounting base into the opening, extend the slides, then screw them to the cabinet bottom at the rear of the cabinet. Install the slides parallel to the cabinet sides, so the base slides back and forth freely.

SECURE UNIT TO MOUNTING BASE WITH 3/4" DRYWALL SCREW

4 Screw the tray unit to the mounting base using 3/4-in. screws. After installing the first screw, slide the unit forward and back, then adjust it until it runs parallel to the cabinet sides and install three more screws.

tips

- Beg, borrow or rent a compressor, finish nailer and brad gun, if you can. You'll work faster, eliminate hammer marks and split the wood less often than you would hand-nailing.
- Test-fit your shelf units in the cabinet as you work.
- Use a damp sponge to wipe up glue drips immediately. It'll save hours of sanding down the line.

Build the swing-out shelf

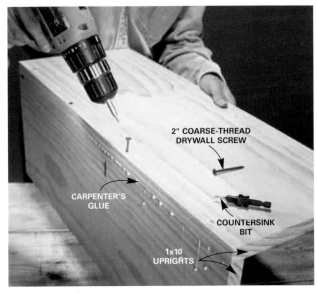

2" COARSE-THREAD DRYWALL SCREW

CARPENTER'S GLUE

COUNTERSINK BIT

1x10 UPRIGHTS

5 Cut the 1x10 swing-out uprights to length and width (one should be 3/4 in. narrower than the other). Use a countersink bit to predrill holes along one edge, then glue and screw the two edges together. The diagonal measurement (see Figure A) should be less than the cabinet opening.

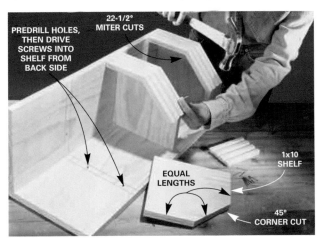

PREDRILL HOLES, THEN DRIVE SCREWS INTO SHELF FROM BACK SIDE

22-1/2° MITER CUTS

EQUAL LENGTHS

1x10 SHELF

45° CORNER CUT

6 Assemble the shelf unit. First mark the shelf positions on the uprights and predrill holes from the front side. Create the three shelves by cutting a 1x10 to length and width, then cutting the corner at 45 degrees. Hold the shelves in place and drive drywall screws through these holes from the back side into the shelves. Cut the 22-1/2-degree angles on the front moldings and secure them with 3d finish nails. You can use any type of wide decorative molding that's at least 1/2 x 3 in.

Figure A
Glide-out and swing-out shelves

- Shelf unit dimensions will vary according to cabinet size.

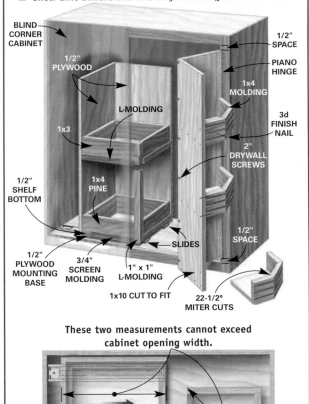

BLIND CORNER CABINET

1/2" PLYWOOD

L-MOLDING

1x3

1/2" SHELF BOTTOM

1x4 PINE

1/2" PLYWOOD MOUNTING BASE

3/4" SCREEN MOLDING

1" x 1" L-MOLDING

1x10 CUT TO FIT

SLIDES

1/2" SPACE

PIANO HINGE

1x4 MOLDING

3d FINISH NAIL

2" DRYWALL SCREWS

1/2" SPACE

22-1/2° MITER CUTS

These two measurements cannot exceed cabinet opening width.

CABINET OPENING WIDTH

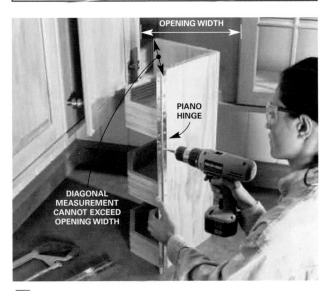

OPENING WIDTH

PIANO HINGE

DIAGONAL MEASUREMENT CANNOT EXCEED OPENING WIDTH

7 Screw the piano hinge to the front edge of the swing-out unit, then to the edge of the cabinet face frame. Make certain the swing-out has 1/2 in. of clearance top and bottom. Use an assistant to help you lift and hold the unit at the proper height while you're securing it to the cabinet.

Sink cabinet shelf

All that wide open space under the sink is a black hole for cleaning products, shoe polish, trash bags—you name it. If you're tired of exploring its depths every time you need something, build this handy door-mounted shelf. Better than store-bought wire racks, it mounts securely, has the same wood finish as your cabinet and maximizes space because you custom-fit it for your cabinet.

The shelf is made from standard 1x4 lumber (which is 3/4 in. x 3-1/2 in.). If you have access to a table saw and have a drill, screwdriver, some wood glue and a tape measure, you can build this project. It takes only a few hours. You can also modify this design to work in other cabinets for holding spices, canned goods or craft supplies.

The shelf has a unique built-in system (Photos 6 and 7) to make mounting it to the back side of a cabinet door a snap. The shelf gets screwed into the solid wood stiles of the door (not into the panel).

Sizing tips

Because there's no standard size for sink base cabinets, here are a few tips to help you size your door-mounted shelf. Measure the height and width of the cabinet opening (Photo 1). The shelf unit must be 1/2 in. less in height and 2 in. less in width (not including the mounting ears shown in Photo 6). These measurements ensure that the shelf unit will clear the frame by 1/4 in. on all sides as you close the cabinet door. Here's how to size each part:

- The height of the 3-1/2-in.-deep sides (A) must be 1/2 in. shorter than the height of the opening.
- The 3-1/4-in.-deep shelves (B) are cut 3 in. shorter than the width of the opening. These pieces are ripped 1/4 in. thinner than the side to allow space for gluing the mounting strips (C) to the back side of the shelves (Photo 4).
- The 1/4-in. x 3/4-in. mounting strips must be 2-1/2 in. longer than B or 1/2 in. shorter than the width of the door opening.

Preparing the sides

After measuring the opening's height and width, cut the sides (A) to length. Then cut a 45-degree taper on the tops of each piece, leaving 3/4 in. at the top as shown in Photo 2. Label the inside of each side so you don't cut the dado (groove) for each shelf on the wrong side. Notice that there are two 1/4-in. notches on the back edge of each side (Photo 2) to accept the mounting strips (C).

To cut the dadoes, set your table saw blade so it's 1/4 in. high. Mark the locations of each dado. The lower dado is on the bottom of the sides, and the top of the upper shelf is 13-1/2 in. from the bottom of the sides.

Cut the dadoes in the inner sides of A using your miter gauge as a guide to push the workpiece through the saw. Our table saw has an extra-wide miter gauge for stability. If your table saw has a small miter gauge, screw a piece of wood to its front edge to extend it to within 1/4 in. of the saw blade. You could make the dado cut in one pass with a special dado blade, but if you don't have one, just make repeated cuts (Photo 2) with a standard blade.

Making the shelves

Cut the shelves (B) to length from 1x4, then rip them to a width of 3-1/4 in. Make the 1/4-in. x 3/4-in. mounting strips (C) and front rails (D) by ripping them from a wider piece as shown in Photo 3.

Before you glue these pieces to the backs of the shelves (Photo 4), drill a 3/16-in. hole 3/8 in. from each end. You'll use these holes later to mount the shelf to the door stiles.

Assembly

Lay out the sides face down as shown in Photo 5. Now slip the shelves with the mounting strips attached into the dadoes and make sure they fit snugly. Drill pilot holes for the screws (3/4 in. from the front and back of A) through the sides into

tip You could make the dado cut in one pass with a special dado blade, but repeated cuts with a standard blade are just as easy for a small project.

the shelves. Use 1-1/4-in. wood screws with finish washers to secure the shelves to the sides.

To finish the assembly, flip the shelves and sides face-up. Cut the 1/4-in. x 3/4-in. front rails (D) to length, drill pilot holes and fasten them (Photo 6) to the front of the sides. We chose to put the lower rail 2 in. up from the bottom shelf and the upper rail 1-1/2 in. up from the upper shelf. These heights work fine for most products and allow you to pull things out instead of lifting them each time. You can always add a second rail just above if needed.

Mounting to the door

Before mounting the unit to the door, apply masking tape to the inside of the door as shown in Photo 7. Close the door and

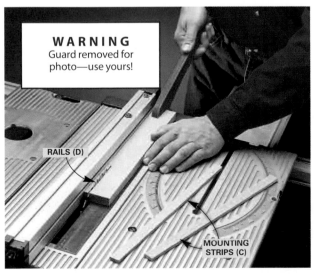

1 Measure the cabinet opening (height and width) to size the shelf system.

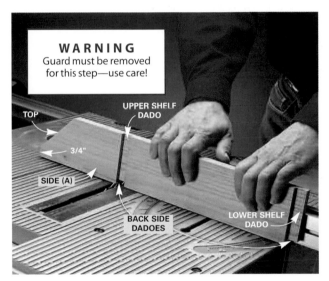

2 Cut the sides (A) to length, then cut the dadoes in the sides and back of each side. See text for dimensions.

3 Rip the mounting strips (C) and the rails (D) from 1x4 lumber.

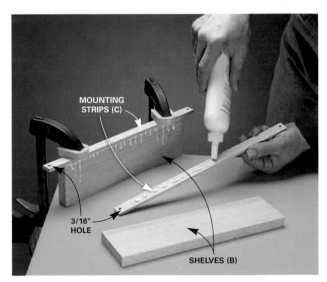

4 Glue the mounting strips (C) to the back side of the shelves. Drill holes in the mounting strips before assembling.

mark the cabinet opening on the tape with a pencil from the inside. This will guide you when you're mounting the shelf to the door. Mount the shelf 1/4 in. from the top mark you made on the tape, and align the ear of the mounting strip 1/4 in. from the opening mark on the door. Mark the holes from the mounting strips onto the door and drill pilot holes for the screws. *Be careful not to drill through the door!* Screw the assembly to the door (Photo 7) using No. 8 x 1-in. screws and finish washers.

Because of the added weight of the shelf and the products, some doors with self-closing hinges may not snap closed as easily as before. To remedy this, you may need to install an extra hinge centered between the other two, or add a magnetic catch at the top of the door.

Remove the shelf from the door, sand it with 150-grit sandpaper, then apply varnish. Shown here are several coats of a clear lacquer spray available at hardware stores. Always apply lacquer in a well-ventilated area away from any pilot flames.
NOTE: If you have small children, be sure that cabinets containing cleaning products have childproof latches attached.

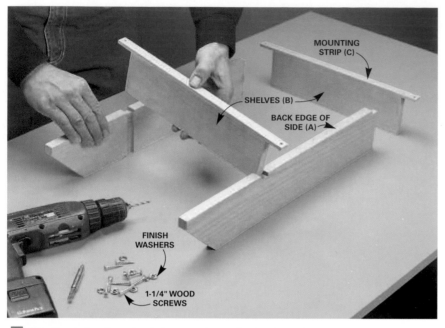

MOUNTING STRIP (C)

SHELVES (B)

BACK EDGE OF SIDE (A)

FINISH WASHERS

1-1/4" WOOD SCREWS

5 Slip the shelves into the dado cuts. Then drill pilot holes into the sides of A and screw the shelves in place with 1-1/4-in. wood screws and finish washers.

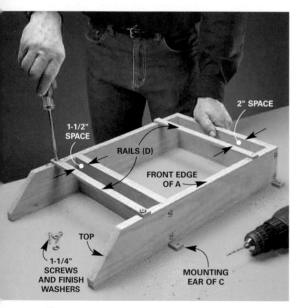

1-1/2" SPACE

2" SPACE

RAILS (D)

FRONT EDGE OF A

TOP

1-1/4" SCREWS AND FINISH WASHERS

MOUNTING EAR OF C

6 Fasten the rails (D) to the front of the shelf assembly. Drill pilot holes and use 1-1/4-in. wood screws and finish washers.

tip You can also modify this design to work in other cabinets for holding spices, canned goods or craft supplies.

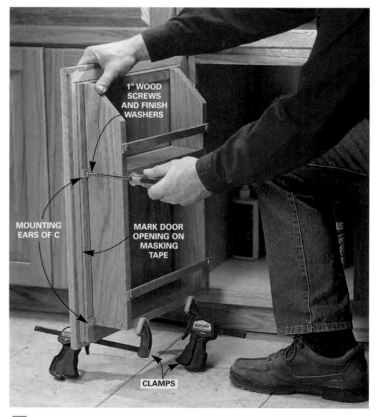

1" WOOD SCREWS AND FINISH WASHERS

MOUNTING EARS OF C

MARK DOOR OPENING ON MASKING TAPE

CLAMPS

7 Clamp and screw the assembly to the door stiles using 1-in. wood screws and finish washers.

Cabinet door message board

A sheet of metal and a whiteboard can turn any cabinet door into a convenient message center. You'll find 2 x 2-ft. lengths of plastic-coated hardboard (sometimes called "dry-erase board") and sheet metal at a hardware store or home center. Larger hardware stores will cut the sheet metal to your specifications. Be sure to get steel instead of aluminum so magnets will stick. Including a can of spray adhesive, this project will cost you less than $20.

If you cut the metal yourself, wear gloves to protect your hands and use tin snips carefully. Use a metal file to smooth any ragged edges. If you don't have a table saw to cut the whiteboard, flip it over, mark your measurements and use a jigsaw to cut it from the back to prevent chipping or splintering. To get a straight cut, use a framing square as a guide (Photo 1).

To mount the metal sheet and whiteboard to the inside of the door, take the door off its hinges, lay it flat and carefully mask off the area where you want to spray the adhesive. Follow the directions on the can to apply the adhesive to the door, metal and whiteboard (Photo 2). Mount the pieces, press firmly and let dry.

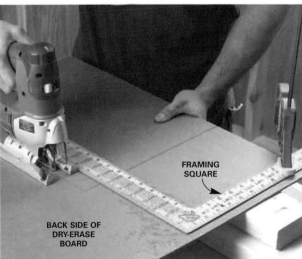

1 Cut the dry-erase board from the back to avoid chipping the plastic-coated face. Use a framing square as a guide to get a straight cut.

2 Spray adhesive onto the door, metal and dry-erase board. Carefully position the metal and board as you stick them to the door—once they're in place, you can't move them.

Fantastic kitchen cabinet rollouts

Rollout trays

Base cabinets have the least convenient storage space in the entire kitchen. Rollouts solve that problem. They make organizing and accessing your cabinet contents back-friendly and frustration free.

If you're stuck with cabinets without rollouts, don't despair. Here you'll learn how to retrofit nearly any base cabinet with rollouts that'll work as well as or better than factory-built units.

It's really very easy. Once you take measurements, you can build the rollout drawer (Photos 2 – 6), its "carrier" (Photos 7 – 9), and attach the drawer slides (Photos 6 and 7), all in your shop. Mounting the unit in the cabinet is simple (Photos 10 – 12). You'll also learn how to construct a special rollout for recycling or trash (Photos 14 – 15).

The project will go faster if you have a table saw and miter saw to cut out all the pieces. A circular saw and cutting

guide will work too; it'll just take a little longer. You can build a pair of rollouts in a Saturday morning for about $20 per pair.

What wood products to buy

These rollout drawers are made entirely of 1/2-in. Baltic birch plywood. Baltic birch is favored by cabinetmakers because it's "void free," meaning that the thin veneers of the plywood core are solid wood. Therefore, sanded edges will look smooth and attractive. If your local home center doesn't stock Baltic birch, find it at any hardwood specialty store.

If you choose, you can make the sides of the rollout drawers from any 1x4 solid wood that matches your cabinets and then finish to match (use plywood for the bases). But if you use 3/4-in. material for the sides, subtract 3 in. from the opening to size the rollout (not 2-1/2 in., as described in Photo 2 and Figure A).

The drawer carriers (Figure A) are made from pine 1x4s for the sides (Photo 7) and 1/4-in. MDF (medium-density fiberboard) for the bottoms (Photo 9). The MDF keeps the drawer bottom spaced properly while you shim and attach it to the cabinet sides. It can be removed and reused for other carriers after installation. If MDF isn't available, substitute any other 1/4-in. hardboard or plywood.

Side-mounted slides are the best choice among drawer slide options. Their ball-bearing mechanisms and precise fit make for smooth-operating drawers that hold 90 lbs. or more. Shown here are 22-in. full-extension KV (800-253-1561; knapeandvogt.com) brand side-mount drawer slides that have a 90-lb. weight rating. That means they'll be sturdy enough even for a drawer full of canned goods. Full-extension slides allow the rollout to extend completely past the cabinet front so you can access all the contents. Expect to pay about $6 to $15 per set of slides at any home center or well-stocked hardware store.

Measure carefully before you build

Nearly all standard base cabinets are 23-1/4 in. deep from the inside of the face frame (Photo 1) to the back of the cabinet. So in most cases, 22-in.-long rollout drawer and carrier sides will clear with room to spare. Check your cabinets to make sure that 22-in. rollouts will work. If you have shallower cabinets, subtract whatever is necessary when you build your rollouts and their carriers (see Figure A).

1 Open the cabinet doors to their widest point and measure the narrowest part of the cabinet opening (usually at the hinges).

FACE FRAME

Figure A
Standard rollout

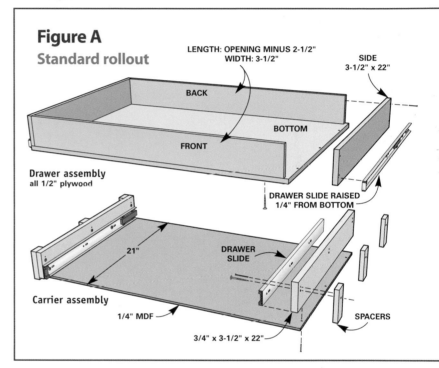

LENGTH: OPENING MINUS 2-1/2"
WIDTH: 3-1/2"

SIDE 3-1/2" x 22"

BACK

BOTTOM

FRONT

Drawer assembly all 1/2" plywood

DRAWER SLIDE RAISED 1/4" FROM BOTTOM

21"

DRAWER SLIDE

Carrier assembly

1/4" MDF

SPACERS

3/4" x 3-1/2" x 22"

Figure B
Wastebasket rollout

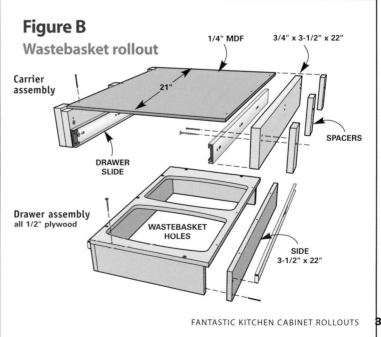

1/4" MDF

3/4" x 3-1/2" x 22"

Carrier assembly

21"

SPACERS

DRAWER SLIDE

Drawer assembly all 1/2" plywood

WASTEBASKET HOLES

SIDE 3-1/2" x 22"

DRAWER FRAME PIECES

3-1/2"

2 Rip 1/2-in. plywood down to 3-1/2 in. wide and cut two 22-in. lengths (drawer sides) and two more to the measured width minus 2-1/2 in. (drawer front and back; Figure A).

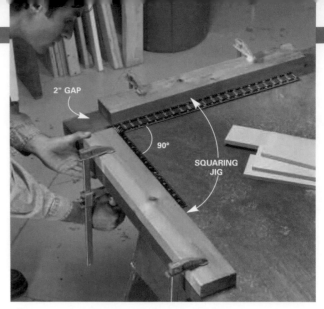

2" GAP

90°

SQUARING JIG

3 Clamp or screw two straight 12-in. 2x4s to the corner of a flat surface to use as a squaring jig. Use a carpenter's square to ensure squareness. Leave a 2-in. gap at the corner.

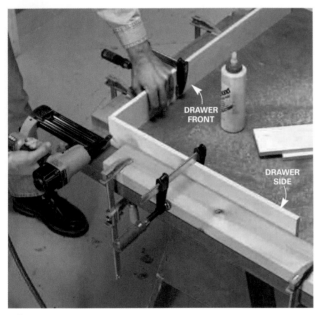

DRAWER FRONT

DRAWER SIDE

4 Spread wood glue on the ends and clamp a drawer side and front in place, then pin the corner together with three 1-1/4-in. brads. Repeat for the other three corners.

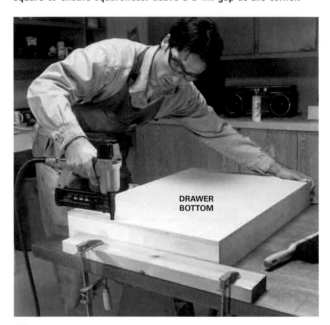

DRAWER BOTTOM

5 Cut a 1/2-in. plywood bottom to size. Apply a thin bead of glue to the bottom edges, and nail one edge of the plywood flush with a side, spacing nails every 4 in. Then push the frame against the jig to square it and nail the other three edges.

Then measure the cabinet width. The drawer has to clear the narrowest part of the opening (Photo 1). When taking this measurement, include hinges that protrude into the opening, the edge of the door attached to the hinges, and even the doors that won't open completely because they hit nearby appliances or other cabinets. Plan on making the drawer front and rear parts 2-1/2 in. shorter than the opening (Figure A).

The project shown here has drawers with 3-1/2-in.-high sides, but you can customize your own. Plan on higher sides for lightweight plastic storage containers or other tall or tippy items, and lower sides for stable, heavier items like small appliances.

Drawer slides aren't as confusing as they may seem

At first glance, drawer slides are pretty hard to figure out, but after you install one set, you'll be an expert. They're sold in pairs and each of the pairs has two parts. The "drawer part" attaches to the rollout while the "cabinet part" attaches to the carrier. To separate them for mounting, slide them out to full length and then push, pull or depress a plastic release to separate the two parts. The cabinet part, which always encloses the drawer part, is the larger of the two, and the mounting screw hole locations will be shown in the directions. (Screws are included with the drawer slides.) The oversized holes allow for some adjustment, but if you follow the instructions, you shouldn't have to fuss with fine-tuning later. When mounting

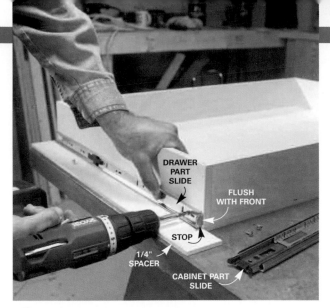

6 Separate the drawer slides and space the drawer part 1/4 in. up from the bottom. Hold it flush to the front and screw it to the rollout side.

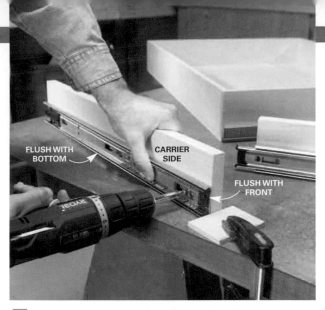

7 Mount the carrier part of the drawer slide flush with the bottom and front of the carrier sides.

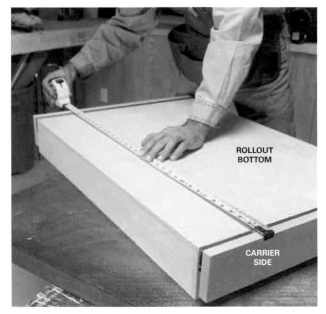

8 Slide the drawer and carrier sides together and measure the carrier width. Cut 1/4-in. MDF to that width and 1 in. less than the carrier depth (usually 21 in.).

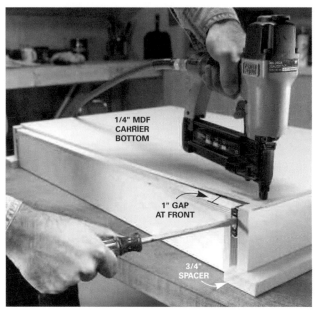

9 Rest the carrier assembly on 3/4-in.-thick spacers, pull the carrier sides slightly away from the drawer, then nail on the carrier bottom (no glue).

the slides, you should make sure to hold them flush with the front of the rollout drawer and carrier sides (Photos 6 and 7). The front of the drawer part usually has a bent metal stop that faces the front of the drawer.

Assembling parts and finishing the rollouts

It's important to build the rollout drawers perfectly square for them to operate properly. Photos 3 and 4 show a simple squaring jig that you can clamp to a corner of any workbench to help. Use the jig to nail the frame together, but even more important, to hold the frame square when you nail on the bottom panel. If it hangs over the sides even a little, the drawer slides won't work smoothly.

Use 1-1/4-in. brads for all of the assembly. Glue the drawer

parts together but not the bottom of the carrier. It only serves as a temporary spacer for mounting. (After mounting the carrier and drawer, you can remove it if it catches items on underlying drawers or even reuse it for other carriers.) If you'd like to finish the rollout for a richer look and easier cleaning, sand the edges with 120-grit paper and apply a couple of coats of water-based polyurethane before mounting the slides.

To figure the spacer thickness, rest the lower carrier on the bottom of the shelf, push it against one side of the cabinet and measure the gap on the other (Photo 10). Rip spacers to half that measurement and cut six of them to 3-1/2 in. long. Slip the spacers between both sides of the carrier to check the fit. They should slide in snugly but not tightly. Recut new spacers if needed. In out-of-square cabinets, you may have to custom-cut spacers for each of the three pairs of

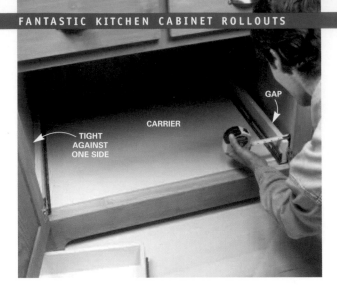

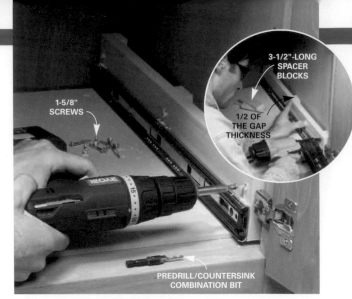

10 Remove the drawer, tip the carrier into the cabinet and push the carrier against one side. Measure the gap and rip six 3-1/2-in.-long spacers to half of the thickness.

11 Nail the spacers to the center and each end of the carrier sides (not into the cabinet; see inset photo). Then predrill and screw the carrier sides to the cabinet in the center of each shim. Slide the drawer back into place.

12 Cut plywood spacers to temporarily support the upper rollout and set them onto the carrier below. Rest the second carrier on the spacers and install it as shown in Photo 11.

13 Build an upside-down version of the carrier and rollouts for the wastebasket drawer (Figure B). Center and trace around the rim of the wastebasket(s). Use a compass to mark the opening 1/2 in. smaller.

spacers, so check each of the three spacer positions. It's easiest to tack the spacers to the rollouts to hold them in place before predrilling 1/8-in. holes and running the screws through the rollout frames and spacers and into the cabinet sides (Photo 11).

Slip the rollout into its carrier and check for smooth operation. If you followed the process, it should work perfectly. If it binds, it's probably because the spacers are too wide or narrow. Pull out the carrier, remove the spacers and start the spacer process all over again.

The best way to level and fasten the upper rollout is to support it on temporary plywood spacers (Photo 12). The photo shows pieces of plywood cut 7 in. high. In reality, the exact height is up to you. If, for example, you want to store tall boxes of cereal on the bottom rollout and shorter items on the

top, space the top rollout higher. You can even build and install three or more rollouts in one cabinet for mega storage of short items like cans, cutlery or beverages. (Those now-obsolete shelves you're replacing with rollouts are good stock to use for your spacers.) Again, pin the spacers in place with a brad or two to hold them while you're predrilling and screwing the carriers to the cabinet sides. Be sure to select screw lengths that won't penetrate exposed cabinet sides! In most cases, 1-5/8-in. screws are the best choice. Strive for 1/2-in. penetration into the cabinet sides. Countersink the heads as far as necessary to get the proper penetration.

Building wastebasket rollouts

Wastebasket rollouts are just upside-down versions of standard rollouts. That is, the carrier is mounted on the top rather than the bottom of the rollout and the slides are positioned at

14 Drill 1/2-in. starting holes and cut the openings with a jigsaw.

STARTING HOLE

15 Mount the wastebasket carrier and drawer as shown in Photos 10 and 11.

the bottom edge of the carrier sides. That lets the wastebasket lip clear the MDF. Follow Figure B on p. 33 for the details.

This wastebasket rollout is built inside an 18-in.-wide cabinet, so it fits two plastic containers back to back. If you only have a 15-in. cabinet to work with, you may be limited to one container mounted sideways. Buy your containers ahead of time to fit your opening.

With some wastebasket rollouts, you may need to knock the MDF free from the carriers after mounting so the wastebasket lips will clear. That's OK; it won't affect operation.

It may not always work to center rollout assemblies in all openings with equal spacers on each side. That's especially true with narrow single cabinets that only have one pair of hinges. It's best to test things before permanent mounting. But if you make a mistake, it's a simple matter to unscrew the assembly, adjust the shims and remount everything.

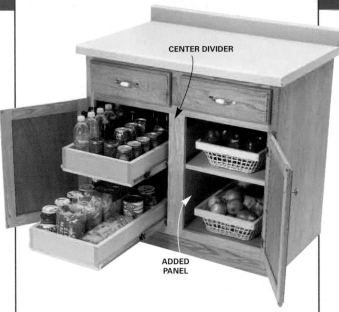

CENTER DIVIDER

ADDED PANEL

Building rollouts in cabinets with center dividers

Many two-door cabinets have a center divider (photo above), which calls for a slightly different strategy. You can still build rollouts, but they'll be narrower versions on each side of the divider. (Check to be sure they won't be so narrow that they're impractical.) The key is to install a 3/4-in. plywood, particleboard or MDF panel between the center divider and the cabinet back to support the carriers.

Cut the panel to fit loosely between the divider and the cabinet back and high enough to support the top rollout position. Center the panel on the back side and middle of the divider and screw it into place with 1-in. angle brackets (they're completely out of sight). Use a carpenter's square to position the panel perfectly centered and vertical on the cabinet back and anchor it there, again using angle brackets. Measure, build and install the rollouts as shown here.

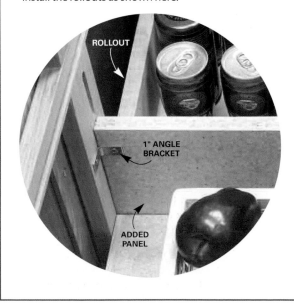

ROLLOUT

1" ANGLE BRACKET

ADDED PANEL

Rollout bins

If you're tired of digging through cans and boxes to find a jar of tomato sauce hidden at the back of the cabinet, these rollout bins are the perfect solution. You can size them to fit inside any lower cabinet and customize them to suit the items you want to store.

Here you'll learn exactly how to build them. The bins are simply plywood boxes with adjustable shelves—very easy to build. Sizing the boxes and mounting them on drawer slides can be tricky, but the techniques shown here make those steps nearly foolproof.

Money, time and tools

All the materials for these three rollouts cost just under $100. You could buy and install a manufactured system, but expect to spend about $80 per rollout.

You don't need advanced cabinet-building skills or tools to make your own rollouts—the joinery and assembly are simple. But a table saw is almost mandatory for fast, accurate, good-looking results. A pneumatic brad nailer will make the job faster and easier, although you can hand-nail or screw the parts together. Ordinarily, the side-mount drawer slides are tricky to install, but this project makes even that step foolproof, so don't let that part intimidate you. You'll be surprised how fast you can build yourself a few rollouts. Put in a full day and you'll be loading them with groceries that evening.

Sizing your rollouts

Everything you need for this project is available at home centers (see the Materials list, p. 40). You'll have to guess at the quantity of rollouts at this point so you can buy the proper number of drawer slides. One sheet of plywood will provide enough material for at least four rollouts. You can roughly figure one rollout for every foot of open base cabinet space you have. You can always return any uncut lumber or hardware you don't use.

To determine the width of your rollouts, gather the items you want to store. Then cut the 1x3 cleats to length and space them from each side of the cabinet with 3/4-in. blocks (Photo 1). That space allows the rollouts to clear the doors and hinges later. Arrange the items you want to store, separating them with the cleats. Leave at least 2-1/2 in. between your items and the cleats. This allows for the clearance of wood thicknesses and drawer slides and 1/2 in. extra to make it easy to load the items and take them out. It takes a bit of rearranging and thought to arrive at the best sizes. If your base cabinets have vertical dividers between the doors, give each opening its own rollouts.

You'll probably have some rollouts facing one way and some the other. That's because rollout access may be blocked by neighboring cabinets at inside corners or because some cabinet doors don't swing all the way open. Determine the access direction while you assemble your rollouts. That's as simple as drilling the finger pull hole at the proper end. After the boxes are assembled, they'll work for either orientation.

Choosing the materials

Choose any 3/4-in. veneered interior plywood for your rollouts. Avoid construction plywood; it won't be as flat and may warp later. If you'd like your rollouts to match your cabinets, choose whatever type of wood does the job. The plywood end grain is sanded on these, but if you'd like a more polished look, buy iron-on edge banding to match the wood type and iron it on after assembling the boxes.

Buy nice, straight, knot-free 1x3s for the cleats—the wood type doesn't matter. Select 22-in. European side-mount drawer slides rated to support 90 lbs. They'll come with their own screws and installation directions that show you how they work.

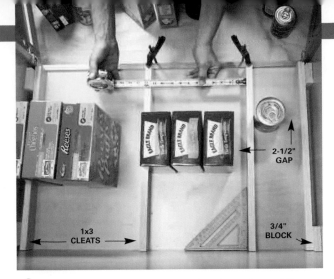

1 Plan rollout widths by laying out the cleats along with the items you want to store. Space the end cleats with 3/4-in. blocks.

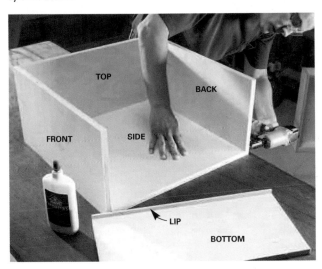

2 Assemble the boxes by gluing and nailing the front, top, back and bottom to the side panel and to each other. Nail the lip to the bottom shelf before assembling.

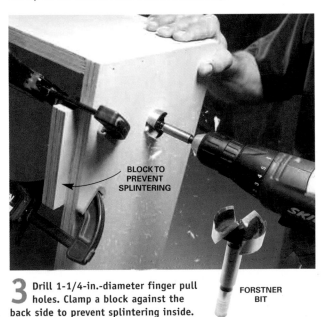

3 Drill 1-1/4-in.-diameter finger pull holes. Clamp a block against the back side to prevent splintering inside.

Materials list

- One 1x3 the width of the cabinet (hold-down rail)
- 2 ft. of 1x3 (drawer slide cleats)
- 8 ft. of 1/4-in. x 1-1/8-in. mullion (base and shelf front lips)
- Four 2-ft. shelf standards with clips
- One pair of 90-lb.-rated full-extension side-mount drawer slides
- 1-1/2-in. pneumatic air nailer brads
- Wood glue
- Small box of 3-in. screws
- 1-1/4-in. Forstner drill (for drilling finger pulls)

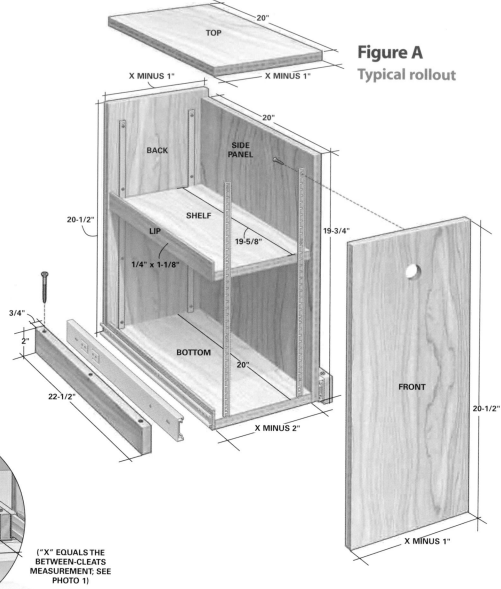

Figure A
Typical rollout

TOP

20"

X MINUS 1"   X MINUS 1"

20"

BACK   SIDE PANEL

SHELF

20-1/2"

LIP

19-5/8"

19-3/4"

1/4" x 1-1/8"

3/4"

2"

BOTTOM

20"

22-1/2"

X MINUS 2"

FRONT

20-1/2"

X MINUS 1"

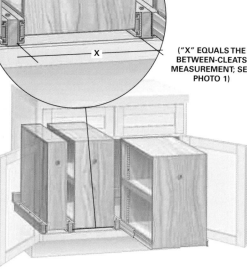

("X" EQUALS THE BETWEEN-CLEATS MEASUREMENT; SEE PHOTO 1)

X

Figure B
Typical rollout grouping

Get more storage space—without remodeling

Lower cabinets offer the biggest storage spaces in most kitchens. But according to kitchen designers, the back half of this space is usually wasted—it's packed with long-forgotten junk or left unused because stored items are out of view and hard to reach. Rollout bins let you see and use the whole space.

Cutting the parts

Most base cabinets are 22-1/2 in. deep and have a 21-in.-high opening (measured inside the face frame, not the cabinet interior). If your cabinets match these measurements, use the height and width dimensions shown in Figure A for all of the side panels. Also use Figure A for the lengths of each top, bottom, front and back panel and shelves. If your cabinets have shorter openings or are shallower, subtract those differences from the Figure A measurements to cut your parts. Calculate the rollout widths based on your layout work inside the cabinet (Photo 1). Subtract 1 in. from the distances between the cleats to get the width for each rollout's top, front and back panel. That'll leave the 1-in. clearance needed for the drawer slides. Subtract 2 in. to establish the width for each bottom panel and the adjustable shelves. That'll leave an additional 1-in. clearance for the thickness of the 3/4-in. side panel and the 1/4-in.-thick lip in the front.

Be especially careful when you lay out the cleats, measure openings and cut the rollout parts. European side-mount drawer slides leave very little room for error. It's best to use a table saw for all of the cuts and to double-check widths and lengths so the boxes will fit together perfectly and engage and operate smoothly in the slides.

Assemble the rollout boxes

Glue and nail the lip on each bottom panel (and shelves) before assembling the rollouts. A thin bead of wood glue on each edge is all you need. Then hold the edges of each panel flush while you pin them together with 1-1/2-in. brads spaced about every 4 in. (Photo 2). Next, drill the 1-1/4-in.-diameter finger pull hole. A Forstner bit will make the neatest hole, but a sharp spade bit will work, provided you use a block on the back side to prevent splintering (Photo 3). The hole defines each rollout's open side.

Cut the 24-in.-long shelf standards down to 18 in. with a hacksaw. Look at the embossed shelf numbers to determine which end is the top and cut from that end. Nail the standards in place with the brads provided (Photo 4).

This is the best time to apply the finish of your choice to the rollouts. Lightly sand everything with 220-grit sandpaper and add the finish. These boxes have two coats of water-based polyurethane to protect the wood against dirty fingers and marks from cans.

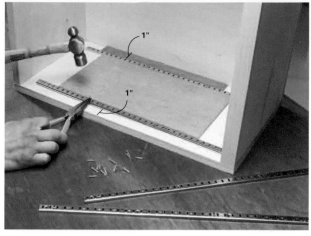

4 Nail shelf standards to the inside of the front and back of each box. Use spacers to position them.

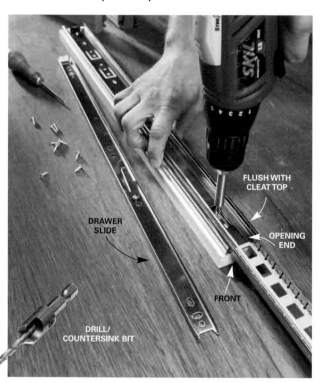

5 Screw the drawer slides to the cleats. Position each slide flush with the front and top of the cleat.

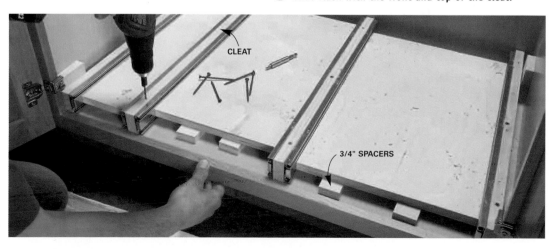

6 Predrill and screw the cleats to the cabinet. Use plywood scraps the same width as the boxes for perfect spacing.

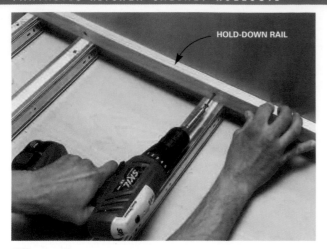

7 Screw the hold-down rail to the cabinet back directly above the cleats with 1-5/8-in. screws.

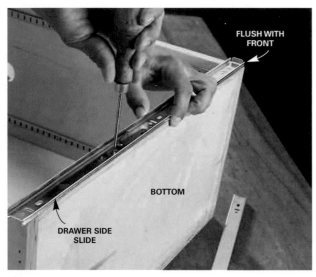

8 Release the drawer slides from the cleat slides and screw them to the side of each box flush with the bottom and the front.

9 Slip the box-mounted slides into the cleat slides and push the box all the way in to fully engage the slides.

Install the drawer slides and cleats

Rip the 1x3s down to 2 in. and then screw on the drawer slides (Photo 5). It's easiest to remove the drawer part of the slide to access the anchor holes. Hold the slides flush with the top and front of each cleat while you punch little starter holes with a scratch awl, and then send in the screws. Drive just one screw at a time so you can adjust the placement as you add screws. You'll need right and left sides for the end cleats. Then remove the drawer side slides and lay the cleats in the cabinet.

Begin with one of the end cleats and press it against the temporary 3/4-in. blocks while you drill three 1/8-in. pilot holes. A combination drill/countersink bit works great for this. Then screw the cleat to the cabinet floor with 3-in. screws (Photo 6). Space the next cleat with a leftover scrap from the first rollout top, front or back. That way the spacing between the drawer slides will be perfectly sized for smoothly operating rollouts. Hold the spacer up from the cabinet floor with 3/4-in. blocks so it'll be centered on the drawer slides. Hold the cleat snug, but not tight, against the spacer while you drill and then screw it to the cabinet floor. Repeat that step with the rest of the cleats. Skip the 3/4-in. blocks on the last cleat and just use the rollout spacer. Screw a 1x3 "hold-down" rail to the back side of the cabinet (Photo 7). It'll help hold the rollout cleats in place when you pull out heavily loaded rollouts.

Finally, disengage the drawer side slides and screw them to the bottom of each rollout flush with the bottom and front (Photo 8). Finish up by inserting each rollout, then load them up!

Manufactured kitchen rollouts

Rollouts are one of the easiest and most satisfying upgrades you can make to your kitchen. They bring everything that's tucked out of sight in the back of cabinets right to your fingertips—you actually gain usable storage space.

Rollouts turn wasted space deep inside cabinets into accessible storage space.

If you don't want to pull out the tools to build your own rollouts, you can shop for moderately priced yet sturdy ones online or at home centers. You simply mount them to the existing shelves in your cabinets with four screws.

The biggest mistake is ordering the wrong size. When you measure the opening in the front of the cabinet, be sure to account for the door, hinges and other obstructions.

This two-level rollout fits around the drainpipes under a sink.

Tips for a tidy bathroom

Bathroom shelving unit

In a small bathroom, every single square inch counts. These shelves make the most of wall space by going vertical. The version shown here, made of cherry, cost about $100. But you can build one for $50 or less if you choose a more economical wood, such as oak or pine. All you need is a 6-ft. 1x4, a 6-ft. 1x6 and a 6-ft. 1x8.

Cut the middle spacers and the shelves 12 in. long. Cut the bottom spacer 11 in. long to allow for a decorative 1-in. reveal. Cut the top spacer to fit (the one shown was 7-1/4 in.). Measure 1 in. from one edge of the backboard and draw a guideline for the shelves and spacers along its length. Nail the bottom spacer in place, leaving a 1-in. reveal at the bottom edge. Center the first shelf by measuring 3-1/4 in. in from the edge of the backboard and nail it in place. Work your way up the backboard, alternating between spacers and shelves (Photo 1).

On the back side, use a 1/8-in. countersink bit to drill two holes, one at the top and one at the bottom of each spacer. Drill two holes spaced 1 in. from each side of the backboard into each shelf ledge. Drive 1-1/4-in. drywall screws into each hole (Photo 2). Paint or stain the assembled unit. If you'd like to clearcoat it, use a wipe-on poly or spray lacquer—using a brush would be really tough. Mount the unit on the wall with two 2 1/2-in. screws and screw-in drywall anchors (E-Z Ancor is one brand). Drive the screws where they won't be seen: right below the bottom shelf and right above the top shelf.

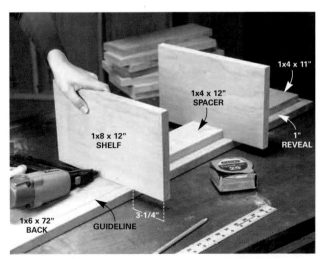

1 Nail the spacers and shelves in place, starting at the bottom and working your way up. Place the bottom spacer 1 in. from the lower edge of the backboard.

1x4 x 11"
1x4 x 12" SPACER
1x8 x 12" SHELF
1" REVEAL
1x6 x 72" BACK
GUIDELINE
3-1/4"

2 Strengthen the shelves by driving screws through the backboard into the shelves and spacers. Drill screw holes with a countersink bit.

Behind-the-door medicine cabinet

The biggest challenge in installing a recessed cabinet is finding unobstructed stud cavities in an open wall. The wall behind the door is usually open, but make sure that pipes, ducts and wiring don't get in the way. To choose the location for the cabinet, begin by finding the studs with a stud finder. Hold the cabinet to the wall at the best height and mark the cabinet near one side of a stud. Find the exact location of that stud by sawing through the drywall until the blade is stopped (Photo 1). Use the cuts to define one cabinet side, and draw the cabinet outline.

Cut out the drywall and then cut off the exposed stud (Photo 2). Add the framing, then screw the cabinet to the framing (Photo 5). Add trim around the edges if necessary to conceal the rough drywall edges.

tip Before you cut a full-size hole in the wall, cut a 6 x 6-in. hole and shine a flashlight inside to check for obstructions.

1 Outline the inset medicine chest to fall against a stud on one side and cut out the opening with a drywall saw.

2 Cut the intermediate stud flush with the drywall on the back side. Push it sideways to release the drywall screws on the back side and remove the stud.

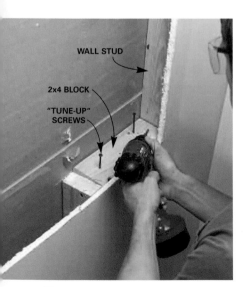

3 Screw blocking to adjacent studs at the top and bottom of the opening. Drive temporary "tune-up" screws into the block to help position it.

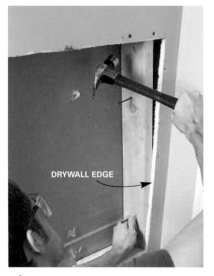

4 Cut and tap in vertical backing flush with the drywall edge, then toe-screw it to the blocking.

5 Slip the cabinet into the opening and anchor it with pairs of 2-in. screws. Add trim if needed.

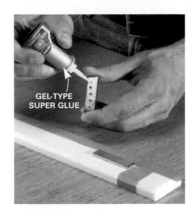

1 Mark the position of the magnets and glue them on the mounting strip, orienting the magnets so they attract each other.

GEL-TYPE
SUPER GLUE

Magnetic toothbrush holder

The problem: Battery-powered toothbrushes don't fit in toothbrush holders and end up lying on a wet, messy countertop.

The solution: Mount neodymium ("rare earth") magnets on a Corian mounting strip with Super Glue. Glue the strip to the wall with Super Glue or silicone caulk.

Tools and materials: To make the mounting strip, cut a Corian threshold ($12 at tile stores) with a miter saw or jigsaw. Neodymium magnets are available from kjmagnetics.com (888-746-7556) and other Internet suppliers. Shown here are 1/2-in. x 2-in. x 1/8-in. magnets, grade N42 ($3.50 each). You can double them up if you need more holding power.

Note: Neodymium magnets are incredibly strong but break if handled roughly. Order several more than you need—shipping is expensive. Also don't handle neodymium magnets if you wear a pacemaker, and never leave them next to your computer. For more safety information, see the "Neo Mag Safety" link at kjmagnetics.com.

2 Glue the mounting strip to the wall with Super Glue, hot-melt glue or silicone caulk.

12"

4-1/2"
MINIMUM

Make any toothbrush stick

Battery-powered toothbrushes have hidden steel parts that stick to magnets. Mount standard toothbrushes by adding a tiny screw or metal washer to the back.

NO. 4 x 3/8"
SCREW

His-and-hers shower shelves

If you need more than shampoo and a bar of soap in the shower, here's how to provide space for all your vital beauty potions: Get a couple of those shelves that are designed to hang from a shower arm and hang them on cabinet knobs. Use No. 8-32 hanger screws ($1) to screw the knobs into studs or drywall anchors.

Tips for a tidy kitchen

VERTICAL PLYWOOD PANEL

CUT SHELF TO NEW LENGTH

DRILL HOLES FOR SHELF PINS

Cookware organizer

Most kitchen base cabinets lack vertical storage space for big, flat cookware, such as cookie sheets and pizza pans. To provide it, just remove the lower shelf, cut a vertical panel of plywood and fasten it at the cabinet bottom with furniture braces and at the top with a strip of wood. Drill holes for the adjusting pins to match the original locations and trim the shelf to length.

Measuring cup hang-up

Free up drawer space by hanging measuring cups inside a kitchen cabinet. Position and mount a wood strip so that the cups will hang between the shelves and allow the door to close completely. Mount a second strip for your measuring spoons, then screw in cup hooks on both strips.

Thyme saver

If your spices are jammed into a drawer with only the tops visible, this nifty rack that slips neatly into the drawer will solve the problem. And it only takes an hour to build. Make it with scraps of 1/4-in. and 1/2-in. plywood.

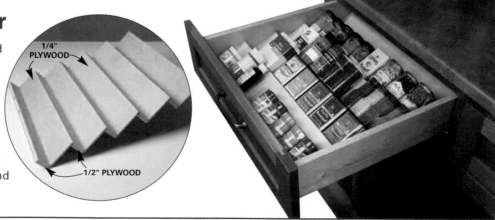

1/4" PLYWOOD

1/2" PLYWOOD

Spice storage

Small spice containers use shelf space inefficiently and are difficult to find when surrounded by taller bottles and items. Use a small spring-tension curtain rod ($3) as a simple shelf. It's easy to install and strong enough to support the spices.

Racks for canned goods

Use those leftover closet racks as cabinet organizers. Trim the racks to length with a hacksaw and then mount screws to the back side of the face frame to hold the racks in place. The back side of the rack simply rests against the back of the cabinet. Now you can easily find your soup and check the rest of your inventory at a glance.

CLOSET ORGANIZER RACKS

ATTACH SCREWS TO BACK SIDE OF FACE FRAME

Wine glass molding

T-molding designed for wood floor transitions makes a perfect rack for stemware. Just cut it to length, predrill screw holes and screw it to the underside of a shelf. For a neater look, use brass screws and finish washers. Prefinished T-molding is available wherever wood flooring is sold. A 4-ft. section costs about $28.

T-MOLDING

FINISH WASHER

Plastic bag dispenser I

An empty rectangular tissue box makes a convenient holder for small garbage bags, plastic grocery bags and small rags. Simply thumbtack it to the inside of a cabinet door.

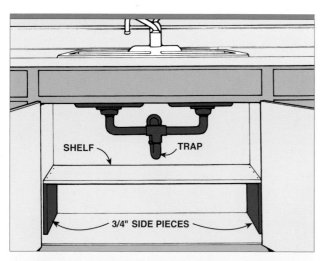

Easy cabinet shelf

Here's a fast-and-easy way to add a shelf to a kitchen cabinet under the sink, or to a bathroom vanity. Cut side supports from 3/4-in. plywood to the height you want, allowing the shelf to fit under the sink trap. Cut the shelf from either 1/2-in. or 3/4-in. plywood, about 1/4 in. shorter than the inside cabinet width. Nail the shelf to the side supports with 6d finishing nails, prime and paint the shelf and sides, and slide the unit in place.

Plastic bag dispenser II

Make it easy to stow and reuse plastic bags with a dispenser made from a discarded 2-liter soda bottle. Cut off the top and bottom with a razor knife. Trim any jagged edges so you don't tear the bags when you pull them out, then screw the dispenser to a cabinet door or closet wall (or attach with hook-and-loop tape).

3 Organize your
workshop

Whether it's in your basement, garage or shed, a workshop is a tough place to keep orderly. All those tools, supplies and hardware—there are never enough drawers or shelves. Don't waste time searching for that certain bit or blade, or money rebuying things you already have but can't find!

We've collected 148 of our very best workshop storage tips, plus we'll show you step by step how to build a clever, two-hour catchall cabinet.

And check out the special section on controlling cords and wires on page 99.

Clever catchall cabinet

Get hanging storage and shelving with this two-hour project

This wall cabinet was designed with painting supplies in mind, but you can use it to store just about anything, including hand tools and small boxes of fasteners and hardware. The build-a-box-and-cut-it-in-half technique is simple and then all you have to do is face-mount a full-length continuous hinge. It couldn't be easier. And the result is a sturdy, practical wall-hung cabinet.

Materials for one of these cabinets cost about $55, but you could reduce the price per cabinet by buying 4 x 8-ft. sheets of pegboard and plywood and building several cabinets instead. Start by cutting 8-in. strips of plywood and screwing them together to form a 2-ft. by 4-ft. box. Place screws accurately as shown in Figure A to avoid hitting them when you cut the box in two (Photo 2). Also be sure to orient the pegboard so the good side faces out on the front and in on the back. Be careful to cut the pegboard pieces perfectly square and with straight sides so you can use them as a guide for straightening the box sides and squaring the box as you nail on the pegboard (Photo 1).

To cut the box into two pieces, begin by tacking a straight board to the box sides as a saw guide. Position the guide so the cut runs 3 in. from the front edge of the box and falls between the screws. Set the saw blade to cut 7/8 in. deep. Align the guide carefully on each side so the cuts meet in the corners. Before you make the final cut, use shims and tape to hold the cabinet together, and keep them on until the cut is complete (Photo 2).

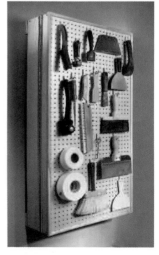

Figure A shows the cabinet dimensions and details as well as the rack to hold paint roller covers. Screw two 3-in.-wide

1 Build a simple box and cover both sides with pegboard. Remember to face the good side of the back pegboard to the inside of the box.

2 Cut the box in two using a guide board for a perfectly straight cut. Before the final cut, use shims and tape to hold the box together.

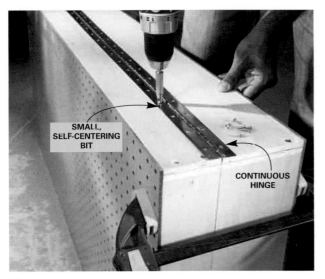

3 Mount the door on the cabinet with a continuous hinge. Hold it in place with one screw on each end. Then use a small, self-centering bit to make pilot holes for the remaining screws.

4 Trim the door with corner molding. Mark the inside of the molding at cabinet corners and turn the molding face down on the miter saw to cut the miter.

strips of 3/4-in. plywood to the back of the cabinet. These provide a stronger hanging surface, and they space the cabinet from the wall to allow the use of pegboard hooks on the cabinet back. Mount the cabinet by driving 1/4-in. by 3-in. lag screws through the hanging strip into wall studs.

Materials list

ITEM	QTY.
4' x 4' x 3/4" plywood	1
2' x 4' pegboard	2
3/4" outside corner molding	14'
1-5/8" screws	24
1-1/2"-wide x 48" continuous hinge	1
48" metal shelf standards	4
Shelf clips	16
Small hook latch	1
1" brads	1 lb.
Wood glue	

You'll also need 3 ft. of closet rod if you want to add the roller cover holder.

Figure A
Cabinet

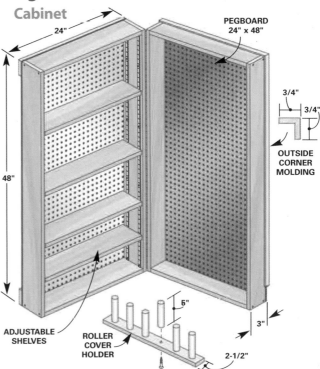

Tips for storing paint, brushes & rollers

Stay-fresh paint storage

Your painting project is done—now what do you do with the unused half gallon of paint? Store it in peanut-butter jars with labels indicating the color and the date used. The paint stays fresh if you fill the jar to the brim, so you won't have to mess with a dried layer of paint during a touch-up job. Plus you can pick the right color in a second without sorting through a shelf load of bulky, rusting gallon cans.

PEANUT-BUTTER JARS

COLOR AND DATE

FILL TO BRIM FOR FRESH PAINT LATER

Out-of-the-way paintbrush storage

Hang your paintbrushes up out of harm's way by installing a couple of screw eyes or cup hooks on the bottom of a couple of rafters or floor joists. Then thread the brush handles through a stiff wire (such as welding rod) and hang it all up.

Self-sealing paint cans

Store paint cans upside down and the paint itself will form an airtight seal around the rim. Make sure the cover is on tight to prevent leakage. Hold the can upright and shake it vigorously before you open it so the solids in the paint drop off the lid.

DRIVE SCREWS
THROUGH SHELF
BOARD INTO LOWER
BOARD'S EDGE

TWO 1x8
BOARDS

SHELF BRACKET

SPRING
CLAMP
BRACKET

Painting gear hangout

Organize your paintbrushes, scrapers, roller frames, rags and paint cans with this shelf made from two 1x8 boards screwed together and reinforced with metal shelf brackets ($1). The shelf shown here is 38 in. long to fit three brackets of sliding spring grips ($4 each at a home center) mounted under the shelf for tool storage.

Airtight finish cans

Glad Press 'n Seal wrap can create an airtight seal on paint and finish cans. There's no need to pound on the metal lid when you feel like calling it quits before the job's done. It's easy to unpeel and reuse sheets if you're feeling especially frugal.

Spray can six-pack

A cardboard six-pack corrals loose spray cans for a neater shop.

9"-PLUS POTATO CHIP CAN

9" PAINT ROLLER

Paintbrush hanger

Here's a handy way to dry and store paintbrushes. Using a handsaw, cut a slanted slice out of the handle from the hole toward the bristles. After cleaning, hook the brush over a coat hanger and hang it from a ceiling joist.

Paint roller storage

When the painting job is half done but the day is *all* done, slide your paint roller off the roller frame and store it in a plastic potato-chip container. It's just the right size for a standard 9-in. roller. Once you've slipped the roller cover inside, pop on the lid, and the wet roller is sealed and ready for service in the morning.

Plastic-wrapped paint roller

You don't have to wash out your paint roller if you'll be using it again tomorrow. Spread a 14-in.-long strip of plastic wrap on a flat surface and push the roller over the plastic. Seal the ends with twist ties.

Tips for storing a tape measure

Tape measure holder

If you've never had a specific place to store your tape measure, you probably can't find it when you need it. Solve this problem by screwing a large sawtooth picture hanger onto the wall behind your workbench. Hook the tape measure onto the hanger and have no trouble finding it in the future .

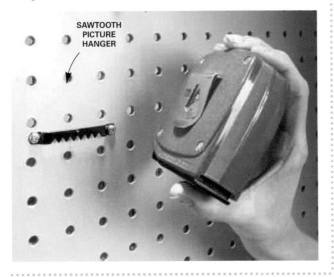

SAWTOOTH
PICTURE
HANGER

Electrical box tool holders

Junction boxes can hold a lot more than switches and wiring. Nail or screw them wherever you need handy holders for small stuff. They come in different sizes and shapes and cost 50¢ to $2 each.

Tape and glasses hanger

A 1/8-in.-thick strip of steel or aluminum fastened to a wall with 3/4-in.-thick spacers makes a great holder for tape measures, safety glasses and other stuff that doesn't hang easily on hooks.

Tips for storing caulk

Snap-in caulk organizer

Make this useful shelf from scraps of plywood and then cut 1-1/2-in. cross sections from a length of 2-in. PVC pipe to hold caulk tubes. Cut a portion out of the pipe section just wide enough so you can flex the pipe section and snap the tubes into place.

Caulk clips

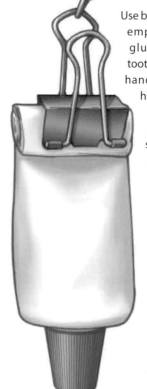

Use binder clips to keep the empty portion of tube glues and caulks (and toothpaste!) rolled up. The handles can be used to hang the tubes for neat, visible storage and flipped alongside the tube to help you squeeze them.

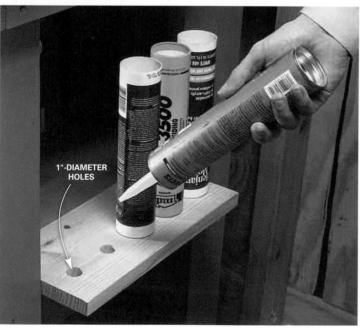

1"-DIAMETER HOLES

Caulk storage shelf

Caulking tubes can be difficult to store—they fall over if you stand them on end and roll away if you lay them flat. Drill 1-in.-diameter holes 2 in. apart in a scrap of wood, and screw the shelf to a flat surface with space below. The weight of the caulk at the tip of the tube keeps it upright.

Taped-up caulk tubes

Here's a slick tip to keep partially used caulk tubes well sealed and at hand. Fold a piece of duct tape over the open tube to seal it, leaving a few inches of extra tape. Drive a nail through the tape and hang the tube on pegboard.

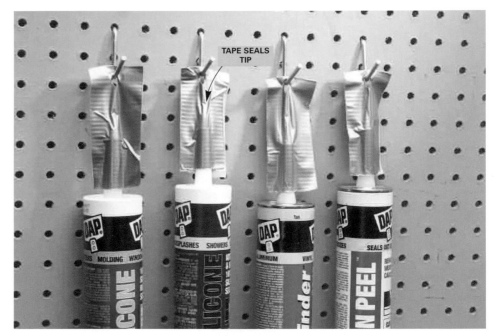

TAPE SEALS TIP

Caulk tube nest

To build this nifty nest, cut 10-in.-long pieces of 2-in. PVC pipe and glue them side to side with PVC cement. To get straight glue lines, use the print along the side of the pipe as a guide. As you glue, hold the pieces together for 60 seconds with hand pressure or a clamp until the glue sets. Be sure to apply the glue only in a well ventilated area. Glue on one tube at a time to fit the available space.

WIPING CLOTHS

GLUE WITH PVC CEMENT

2" PVC, 10" LONG

Hung-up caulk tubes

Here's a great way to store and preserve partially used caulk tubes. Seal the tube by twisting a screw eye or hook into the nozzle, then hang it on a nail or pegboard. Use 3/16-in.- or 3/8-in.-diameter screw eyes or hooks depending on the size nozzle opening you like. The screw threads create a nearly airtight seal by burrowing into the plastic nozzle, but you can reinforce the seal by wrapping electrical tape around the nozzle.

Tips for storing bits & blades

Pie plate storage pockets

Screw cut-in-half pie tins and heavy-duty paper plates to a shop wall and you've got space-saving storage for the sanding discs, circular saw blades and abrasive discs that like to hide in a drawer. Be sure to tape the sharp edges on the cut pie plates to protect your fingers!

Saw blade carryall

This is an oldie but goodie for storing and toting table and circular saw blades. Cut a 14-in. x 12-in. piece of 3/4-in. plywood and drill a hole for a 2-in. x 3/8-in. carriage bolt. Secure the blades on the bolt with a fender washer and wing nut, being careful to stagger the carbide teeth so they don't rub together. Saw a slot in the upper end for a handle and for storing it on pegboard.

SAW OUT FOR HANDLE

3/4" PLYWOOD

3/8" CARRIAGE BOLT

Medicine-bottle bit holder

Keep those little driver bits (and your chuck key) corralled and handy by storing them in a tamper-resistant medicine bottle. Put a screw eye on the cap, then attach the bottle to your screw gun or tool belt with a snap hook.

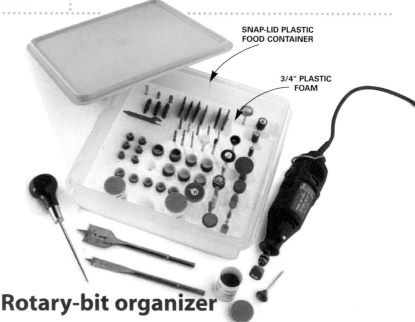

SNAP-LID PLASTIC FOOD CONTAINER

3/4" PLASTIC FOAM

Rotary-bit organizer

This rotary-bit organizer may just inspire a renaissance of rotary tool use in your shop. Friction-fit a piece of 3/4-in. plastic foam in a snap-lid plastic food container. Then poke holes in the plastic foam with an awl to hold shafted bits, and slice crevices with a utility knife to hold cutoff discs. Using a spade bit at high speed, drill sockets for larger bits and tube-shape containers. Once your bits are in order, you can rediscover how useful they can be.

Magnetic bit rack

Mount an 18-in. Magnetic Tool Holder (No. 81281) to your drill press's pulley cowl for quick-change bit storage. (It's available for $18 from rockler.com or by calling 800-279-4441.) The tool holder is inlaid with powerful magnetic strips that tightly hold all sizes of bits, plus it's easy to mount. Mark and drill

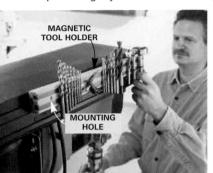

MAGNETIC TOOL HOLDER

MOUNTING HOLE

a couple of 1/4-in. holes through the cowl of your drill press. Then use two 1-1/4 in. x 1/8-in.-diameter bolts with nuts and washers to attach the holder.

While you're ordering, buy a few extra magnetic tool holders and use them elsewhere in your shop to hold chisels, squares, router bits, metal rulers, wrenches and all those easy-to-misplace accessories.

Drill bit rack

Here's the Cadillac of drill bit racks. It comes with a sizing index to check round workpieces and the bits themselves for drilling the exact corresponding hole. The length of the rack is up to you—build it to hold all your bits in order of size. You can either build it freestanding for tabletop use or without the base pieces for wall mounting.

To build one, lay your bits—spade and/or twist bits—on a table with 1/2-in. spacing. Cut two 3/4-in. x 3/4-in. strips of hardwood, then mark, clamp and drill according to the bit spacing you determined. (Drill through

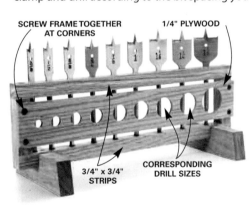

SCREW FRAME TOGETHER AT CORNERS

1/4" PLYWOOD

3/4" x 3/4" STRIPS

CORRESPONDING DRILL SIZES

both strips for spade bits but only halfway through the second strip for twist bits.) Position two 2-3/4-in. blocks between the strips and screw them together. Use the bits you laid out to drill holes in a piece of 1/4-in. plywood for the sizing index. Screw it to the rectangle and get those bits in order!

Bandsaw blade hangers

If you've ever suffered the indignity—and possible danger to eyes and face—of a bandsaw blade uncoiling as you've pulled it off the peg you hung it on, you'll love this tip. Nest the coiled blades into binder clips and store them on your pegboard, and they'll never spring out at you again. Apply labels to the clip so you can simplify size selection and storage.

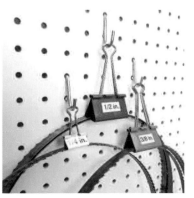

1/2 in.

1/4 in.

3/8 in.

NOTCHES CUT TO SEPARATE BLADES

5/8" DOWEL

Saw blade roost

Here's a double-duty holder for storing and cleaning table saw and circular saw blades. It features a slotted dowel to keep stored blades spaced apart so the teeth stay sharp.

Using a handsaw, cut notches spaced at 3/8-in. intervals halfway through a 5/8-in. dowel. Glue the dowel in a hole drilled in a 16 x 12-in. piece of 3/4-in. plywood. Frame the sides and lower edge of the plywood with 2-in. strips of plywood and add a lower facing piece to create a basin at the bottom.

When a blade needs cleaning, remove the other blades and line the rack with aluminum foil. Then mount the gunked-up blade on the dowel, spray one side with oven cleaner, and flip it over and spray the other side. Any drips go in the basin, and the sides minimize overspray. Let the cleaner work for an hour or so, then use a moistened kitchen scrub pad to scour the dissolved gunk and burned sawdust off the blade. Then throw away the foil and store your blades.

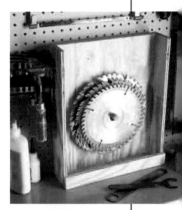

ALUMINUM FOIL

Tips for storing tape, glue & string

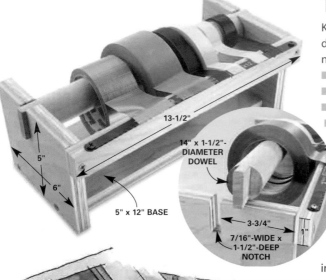

Tape caddy I

Keep your tape rolls easy to use and all in one place with this plywood dispenser. When you run out of tape, just lift the dowel out of the notches, reload and slide it back in the notches. You'll need:

- Two 5-in. x 6-in. side pieces of 3/4-in. plywood
- One 5-in. x 12-in. plywood base
- One 1-in. x 13-1/2-in. hacksaw blade support
- One 14-in. x 1-1/2-in.-diameter dowel rod
- An 18-tooth, 12-in. hacksaw blade

Notch the sides to the dimensions shown and screw them to the base along with the hacksaw blade support.

Saw the dowel ends to fit in the notched sides and screw the hacksaw blade on the support, positioning it so the saw teeth extend a little beyond the edge of the plywood. That's it. Load up with tape and you'll never go hunting for stray rolls again.

P.S. You may want to screw the dispenser to your workbench to aid in pulling tape (especially duct tape) off the roll.

String dispenser I

Prevent balls of twine from tangling up by making a twine dispenser from an empty plastic detergent jug. Cut the bottom off the jug and drill a hole in the cap. Screw the jug to your shop wall with the spout facing down. Drop the ball of twine into the jug, thread it through the hole and screw the cap on.

CD DISPENSER

Reel good storage

The underside of the basement stairs is a great place to store stuff that can be put on a reel: rope, chain, extension cords, Christmas lights, even duct tape. Just drill two small (1/2-in. or so) holes in the stair supports, and run a metal rod or dowel through the holes.

String dispenser III

Using a ball of string or twine can be awkward, especially when you pull on the end and the ball rolls out of your hand and halfway across the floor. Here's an idea to make it easier. Use a CD dispenser and stick the ball of string right on the spindle. Drill a hole into the top of the plastic cover, run the string out of the hole and you've got an easy way to control exactly how much string you take each time.

String dispenser II

Keep your string easily accessible and tangle free with this string holder. Take an old plastic peanut butter jar and drill a hole in the bottom of it. Place a ball of string inside and pull the end of the string through the hole. Fasten the lid to the wall or cabinet near your workbench, and screw the jar onto the lid.

The bottle is full

Is your glue bottle half full or half empty? If every time you need to squeeze a little glue, you've got to wait for it to find its way down to the tip, here's a solution: Now no matter how much glue is in the bottle, it will seem like it's full because the bottle is upside down in this handy stand. To make it, take a 3 x 3-in. block of wood and drill a 1-1/4-in. hole in the middle a little deeper than the wide part of the cap. Then drill a 5/8-in. hole for the neck as shown.

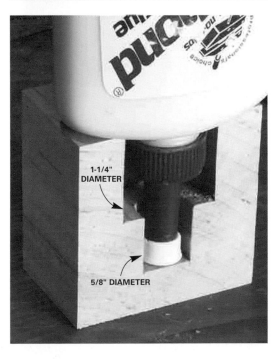

1-1/4"
DIAMETER

5/8" DIAMETER

Glue-go-round

Here are three good reasons to build this glue caddy for your shop. First, no more hunting for the right type of glue; they'll all be right at your fingertips. Second, you can store the containers upside down. That keeps the glue near the spout—no more shaking down half-filled bottles. Third, upside-down storage helps polyurethane glues last longer without hardening because it keeps the air out.

Here's how to make yours:

Arrange all your glue bottles in a circle with 1-in. spacing between the bottles. Add 2 in. to the circle diameter and cut out two 3/4-in. plywood discs. Drill 7/8-in. holes in the center of each one. Measure the various bottle diameters and drill storage holes around the top disc a smidgen larger than the bottles. Glue the discs on a 12-in.-long, 7/8-in. dowel, with a 5-in. space between the discs.

Add a knob of your choice, load up your glue and you've got an instant grip on every type of sticky problem that comes your way.

Tape caddy II

An old toilet paper holder makes a handy tape dispenser for the shop. You can use a surface-mounted holder or a recessed version.

Tips for storing long stuff

Lattice rack

Plastic lattice works well for storing long lengths of miscellaneous pipe, trim, flashing and conduit. Just cut matching pieces, then screw 2x4 cleats to the ceiling and screw the lattice to the wall studs and cleats. Now you can quickly find those oddball leftovers instead of going to the hardware store and buying yet another piece.

Up, up and away

Put those joist spaces to use with this simple storage idea. Fasten eye screws to the joists and then cut lengths of chain to keep odd lengths of trim and pipe out of the way but easy to find. Open one side of the eye screw with pliers to slip the chain in place. Make the chain a bit longer for easy future expansion.

Gutter shelving

Use vinyl rain gutters to store long, thin items, such as molding, light lumber, pipe and certain tools. Lengths of gutter are inexpensive and will support a surprising amount of weight if you brace them with wraparound gutter brackets. Just screw the brackets to the studs of your garage or basement and snap the gutters in place.

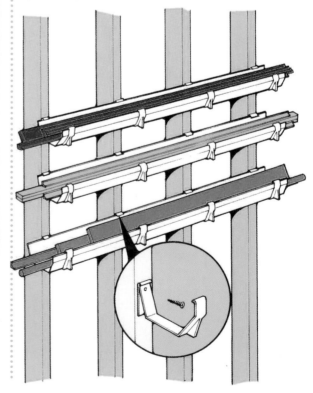

Plywood rack for dowels

Here's a sturdy rack for storing and organizing wood dowels. Use a hole saw to drill 2-1/2-in.-dia. holes in three sheets of 1/4-in.-thick plywood. Screw or clamp the plywood pieces together at the corners so the holes will line up. Then screw the pieces to your shop wall or ceiling. If necessary, a 3/4-in.-wide strip of wood makes a strong bracket for both holding the plywood and securing the units to the wall.

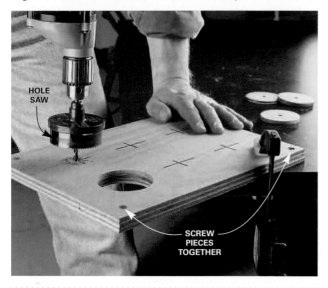

HOLE SAW

SCREW PIECES TOGETHER

WOOD STRIPS

High-rise dowel storage

Organize all the far-flung sticks, dowels and molding scraps in your shop with one 10-ft. length of 3-in. square plastic downspout ($6 at home centers). Cut two 30-in. pieces to hold uncut dowels, two 20-in. pieces to store cut-offs, and two 8-in. pieces for shorter stubs. With a jigsaw, cut away the top 8 in. on one side of the 30- and 20-in. pieces so you can slide sticks in and out more easily. Glue the downspout pieces together with contact cement, then screw together a bottom from 1/2-in. plywood and 1x2s to form a curb. Attach the curb to the downspouts with 3/4-in. sheet metal screws. Screw the whole unit to a shop wall, and put your sticks in order.

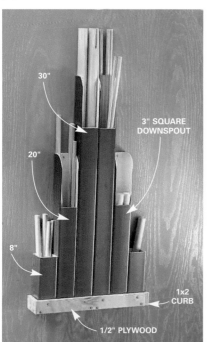

30"

20"

8"

3" SQUARE DOWNSPOUT

1x2 CURB

1/2" PLYWOOD

Oversized twist ties

Leftover scraps of electrical cable can tie up or tie down just about anything. Twist a loop in the cable to make carrying or hanging up your bundle easier.

CARRYING LOOP

Overhead storage

Stow bulky items overhead by cementing together a simple rack from 2-in. PVC pipes and fittings. Bolt the straight pipe to the ceiling joists to support heavy loads, and screw the angled pieces from the "wye" connectors into the cross brace to stabilize the whole rack. The PVC's smooth surface makes for easy loading and unloading.

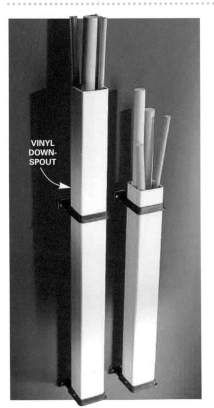

Dowel holsters

An 8-ft. length of vinyl down-spout ($6 at home centers) will make enough dowel holsters to bring law and order to the wildest shop. And the vinyl brackets (about $1 each) made to hold down-spouts to houses make holster-to-shop-wall attachment a snap.

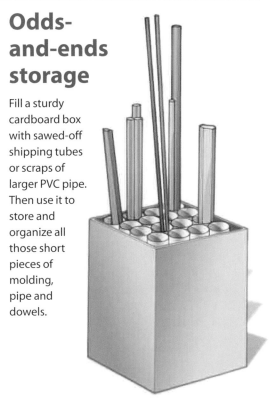

Odds-and-ends storage

Fill a sturdy cardboard box with sawed-off shipping tubes or scraps of larger PVC pipe. Then use it to store and organize all those short pieces of molding, pipe and dowels.

Tips for storing power tools & accessories

Table saw basket

Here's a solution for keeping all your table saw paraphernalia—push sticks, miter fence, extra blades, wrenches—in easy reach and free of sawdust. Attach a plastic storage basket under one side of the saw table with four pieces of stout, vinyl-coated wire. Table saw designs vary, but most have predrilled holes in the wing edges, and you may be able to temporarily loosen a couple of bolts under the table, as shown here, to twist the wire on and retighten the bolts to hold it. For best storage, add a plywood shelf or two, drilled out with a large spade bit so it won't collect dust. Attach the shelves with 3/4-in. screws through the plastic into the plywood.

Cordless drill-driver station

Store cordless drill drivers near their chargers so you won't forget to charge them. Best of all, with their own little roost, your drill-drivers will always be where you can find them.

To make one, rip 3/4-in. plywood into 8-1/2-in.-wide strips. Make your drill-driver station wide enough to hold all your drivers. Cut slots in the lower shelf to fit the driver handles, then glue and nail the station together. Screw the station to a wall near an electrical outlet.

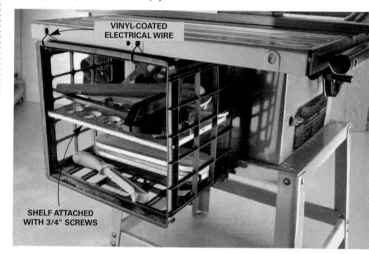

VINYL-COATED ELECTRICAL WIRE

SHELF ATTACHED WITH 3/4" SCREWS

Broom holder for lathe tools

If your lathe tools are always getting buried in a pile of chips or rolling—point first—off the bench, here's a clever solution. Snap lathe-turning tools into spring-loaded broom handle clamps ($4 for a four-clamp bracket at a home center) mounted within easy reach of the lathe. Your lathe tools are now securely stored and easy to see and grab. This device also helps you practice the Zen of returning each tool to its clamp before selecting the next one!

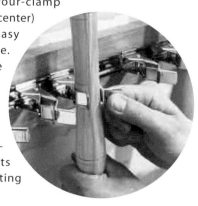

SPRING-LOADED BROOM HANDLE HOLDERS

In-the-bucket air tools

A 2-1/2-gallon bucket is all you need to store air tools and hoses on a wall right by the air compressor. Screw a 3/4-in. plywood shelf inside the bucket to create two storage areas, then attach the bucket to the wall with a couple of lag bolts and washers. Load up the bucket with nailers, nails, tire pressure gauges and other accessories and coil the hose around it.

Drill holster

Avoid the sickening crunch—and possible damage—that happens when your cordless drill falls off a crowded workbench. Screw a 3-in. plastic adapter ($2 in a home center's yard drainage aisle) to the side or back edge of your workbench, and holster that tippy drill. Three-inch drainage adapters hold cordless and corded drills, so buy as many adapters as you have drills to keep them toppleproof and easy to grab.

Cordless drill hangout

Here's a high-and-mighty way to prevent cordless drills from toppling off your workbench. Screw large vinyl-covered hooks (available for $1 at hardware stores and home centers) to a convenient spot on a wall or exposed stud and hang up those drills for safekeeping and easy access.

Air compressor on a roll

Here's a smart way to mobilize your air compressor and neatly store air nailers, nails and air hoses on board. This trolley's dimensions fit a standard, pancake-style compressor, but you can easily adapt the dimensions if you have another style.

To build one, you'll need:

- Two 2 x 4-ft. sheets of 3/4-in. plywood
- Scraps of 1/2-in. plywood
- 1-1/4-in. x 3-ft. dowel
- Four 3-in. swivel casters with brakes and miscellaneous hardware

Cut the 18-in. square floor from 3/4-in. plywood and screw two 4-in.-wide pieces of 3/4-in. plywood under it to attach the casters to them. Cut the side risers from 3/4-in. plywood and screw them to the floor. Then cut the front and back pieces from 1/2-in. plywood and screw them together to box in the compressor. Build the tool storage box on the risers with a 3/4-in. floor and 1/2-in. sides, adding a 3/4-in. plywood partition to organize nailer and fastener storage.

Drill 1-1/4-in. holes in the ends of the risers, then screw and glue in the dowel, leaving a protruding end for keeping the hose on board. Add a 3/4-in. plywood disc to the end of the handle for hose storage. Attach the casters with 1/4-in. x 1-in. lag screws, set the compressor inside, load up the storage box and head for the project at hand.

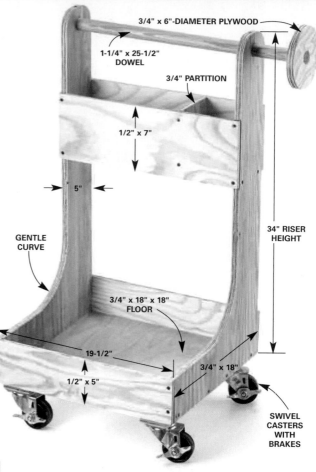

3/4" x 6"-DIAMETER PLYWOOD

1-1/4" x 25-1/2" DOWEL

3/4" PARTITION

1/2" x 7"

5"

34" RISER HEIGHT

GENTLE CURVE

3/4" x 18" x 18" FLOOR

19-1/2"

3/4" x 18"

1/2" x 5"

SWIVEL CASTERS WITH BRAKES

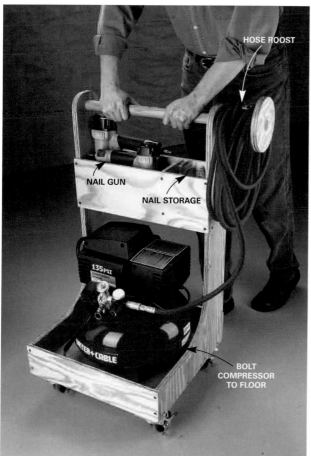

HOSE ROOST

NAIL GUN

NAIL STORAGE

135 PSI

PORTER+CABLE

BOLT COMPRESSOR TO FLOOR

Air hose station

Keep your air hose and fittings in one place and out of the way. Screw a coffee can onto a scrap piece of plywood. Attach a 2-1/2-in. riser block to the edge of the plywood and hang the entire contraption from a wall or workbench. Drape your air hose over the coffee can, and store your fittings inside. It also works great for hanging extension cords.

2-1/2" RISER BLOCK

SNUBBER HOSE

2x2 LIP

DRAIN ACCESS HOLE

Air compressor loft

Nestle your compressor into a corner of the floor and measure the size of the shelf you need to fit it. Leave an extra 2 in. of room at the front where you can screw on a 2x2 lip to "corral" the compressor so it won't walk over the edge while it's running. Then measure the height of the compressor to determine the proper distance from the ceiling to the shelf so the compressor has enough clearance.

To build the shelf, start by fastening 2x6 ledger boards to the studs with 5/16-in. x 4-in. lag screws driven into each stud.

Screw down a chunk of 3/4-in. plywood on top of the 2x6s for the compressor floor and another chunk on the underside for a storage shelf. A strategically placed 3-in. hole makes it easy to drain the tank from underneath. To really complete this air-tool station, solder 1/2-in. copper tubing and attach it to the compressor with a swivel "snubber" hose. Connect an air-hose reel for compact hose storage for long-distance needs and a curlicue-style hose for air-at-your-fingertips bench work.

Easy-to-access cordless tool chargers

Mount charger stands for your cordless tools on scrap pieces of pegboard and hang them on a pegboard wall. Just pull one out for charging, or plug it into a power strip under the pegboard and charge batteries right on the pegboard. Most chargers have mounting holes or keyhole slots on the bottom. For those that don't, use a large hose clamp ($2 at a hardware store) to mount them.

HOSE CLAMP

Circular saw luggage

An old bowling ball bag makes a great portable home for your circular saw. The saw easily slides in and out of the zippered opening, so there's no more coaxing it into that molded plastic case and fumbling with those stubborn plastic snaps. And there's plenty of room for spare blades, a rip guide and the blade-changing wrench. So, if you're spending more time building frames than bowling them, nab a secondhand bag for a couple of bucks at a yard sale or secondhand store.

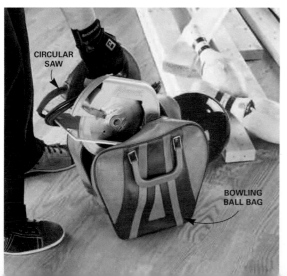

CIRCULAR SAW

BOWLING BALL BAG

Cordless drill holster

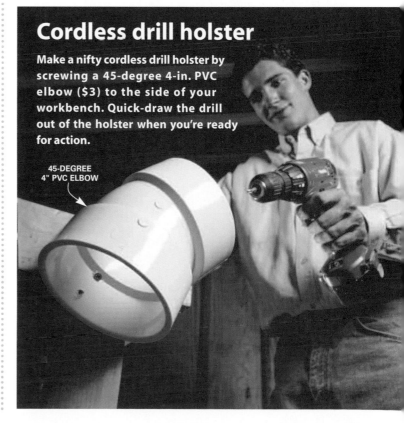

Make a nifty cordless drill holster by screwing a 45-degree 4-in. PVC elbow ($3) to the side of your workbench. Quick-draw the drill out of the holster when you're ready for action.

45-DEGREE 4" PVC ELBOW

Tips for storing a shop vacuum & accessories

BUCKET SPINS 360° WITHIN FRAME

All-aboard shop vacuum

Longing for a shop vacuum that won't tip over, stores the hose between jobs, and carries extra nozzles and cleaning products right on board? Here it is: a plywood carryall made from scrap 1/2-in. and 3/4-in. plywood. The bucket spins 360 degrees in the frame like the turret on an army tank. Use these dimensions as a guide and adjust them to fit your vacuum.

First, screw together a 10-in.-high plywood frame 1/4 in. larger than the bucket's diameter. Cut ovals in the 1/2-in. sides for handles. Screw the frame to a 1/2-in. plywood floor, leaving extra space around three sides for storage.

Next, drill holes in short pieces of 3/4-in. plywood to hold pieces of PVC pipe to store the hose and nozzles. Use 1-1/2-in. PVC for a 2-in.-diameter hose. A 1-7/8-in. hole saw creates tightly fitting holes for the pipe. Now screw swiveling wheels under the floor and get to work cleaning your shop or car.

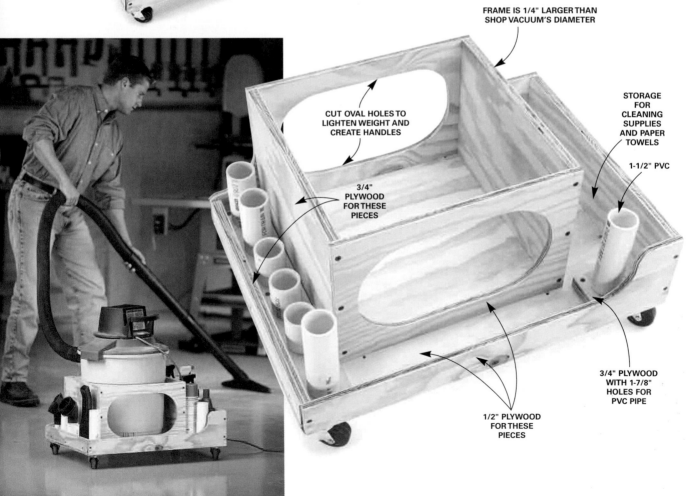

FRAME IS 1/4" LARGER THAN SHOP VACUUM'S DIAMETER

STORAGE FOR CLEANING SUPPLIES AND PAPER TOWELS

1-1/2" PVC

CUT OVAL HOLES TO LIGHTEN WEIGHT AND CREATE HANDLES

3/4" PLYWOOD FOR THESE PIECES

3/4" PLYWOOD WITH 1-7/8" HOLES FOR PVC PIPE

1/2" PLYWOOD FOR THESE PIECES

Shop vacuum attachment holder

Take one of your shop vacuum attachments to a home center and find a PVC tee that fits. Drill a hole in the tee large enough to accept a screwdriver, place a small plywood spacer behind it and screw it to the wall.

1/2" PLYWOOD SPACER

Shop vacuum tool storage

A simple way to store all the nozzles and hoses for your shop vacuum is to drill a 3/16-in. hole in each of them, no more than an inch from the end, then hang them up on pegboard. The holes are sealed up when you attach the nozzles to the hose.

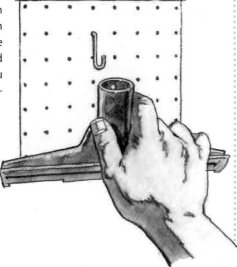

Store shop vacuum attachments

It's aggravating to go hunting for your shop vacuum attachments when you have a mess to clean up. Keep track of these parts by attaching them to the canister with Velcro strips.

VELCRO STRIPS

Well-stowed shop vacuum hose

Loop a Velcro strip ($2 a pack at home centers) on the vacuum's handle and another on the end of the hose. Now that hard-to-tame hose will stay neatly coiled.

HOOK-AND-LOOP FASTENERS

Tips for storing clamps

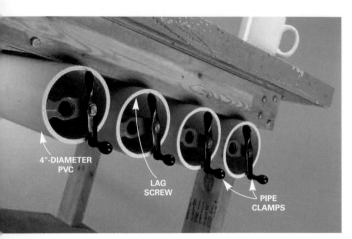

4"-DIAMETER PVC   LAG SCREW   PIPE CLAMPS

Pipe clamp quivers

A great way to store pipe clamps is in pieces of 4-in. dia. PVC pipe screwed under your work table. The PVC costs $4 for a 10-ft. length. To secure the pipes, use 2-in. lag screws and a socket wrench with a ratchet drive to allow you to reach in the end of the pipes and tighten them.

BACKER BOARD

6"

SPACE BLOCKS 1/8" WIDER THAN PIPE O.D.

2x4 BLOCK

Rugged-and-ready pipe clamp rack

With this sturdy, easy-to-build pipe clamp rack, there's no fuss when you're hanging up the clamps, and they're just as easy to take down when you need them. Plus the generous width and depth of the 2x4 won't let a clamp fall off the rack if you bump the bottom end.

Build the rack from scrap pieces of 2x4 and a 3/4-in.-thick backer board of whatever length you need. Cut 6-in. lengths of 2x4, with 45-degree corners on the bottom ends so it's easier to slide the clamps into the rack. Measure the O.D. (outside diameter) of your pipes, then add 1/8 in. for clearance between blocks. Space and screw the 2x4s along the backer board, creating gaps 1/8 in. wider than the pipe's outside diameter. Finally, screw the backer board to the wall and load it up!

Pipe clamp cradle

This handy under-mount rack keeps your clamps right where you need them. Simply cut a series of 1-1/4-in.-diameter holes along the center line of a 2x6 and then rip the 2x6 in half to create the half-circle slots. Next, screw 1x4 sides and a top to the cradle and screw it to the bottom of your workbench.

SIDE   1x4

SIDE

1x4

TOP

PVC pipe clamp rack

Are your pipe clamps missing in action right when you need them? Never again, thanks to this slick snap-in, snap-out storage rack, made from PVC pipe. For 1/2-in.-diameter iron pipe, use 3/4-in. PVC, and for 3/4-in.-diameter pipe use 1-in. PVC.

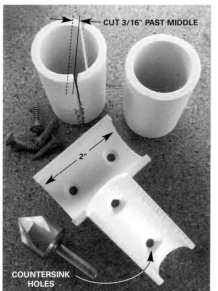

To make the rack, cut 2-in. lengths of PVC, and with a hacksaw or band saw, slice them lengthwise about 3/16 in. past the diameter's center line. This creates the gripping action to firmly hold the heavy iron pipe. Drill and countersink two holes in each PVC piece, then space and screw them along a pair of 2-in.-wide boards. Attach the upper board to your shop wall and snap a pipe clamp in either end to position the lower board for screwing to the wall. That's it. You've shaped AWOL pipe clamps into an orderly arsenal.

Pipe clamp hanger

Since the caps that cover the ends on home-center pipe screw tightly on the threads, you can use them to store your pipe clamps on a shop wall. Drill holes in the top of the caps, tighten eye bolts in the holes with nuts on both sides, then attach them to your clamps and hang them up.

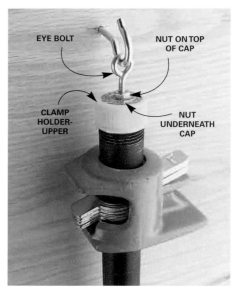

Pipe clamp pincushion

Here is a slick way to store pipe clamps. Cut two 12 x 16-in. pieces of 3/4-in. plywood and temporarily screw or nail them face to face. Drill 1-1/4-in. holes (if your pipes are 1 in. outside diameter), spaced 3 in. apart, through both pieces. Pry the plywood apart, then screw them to two 16-in.-long pieces of 2x8 to make an open-ended box. Add a couple of narrow 3/4-in. boards on the bottom for feet, then set the box in a convenient spot along a shop wall. To keep it from sliding, attach it to the studs with screws driven through the 2x8s.

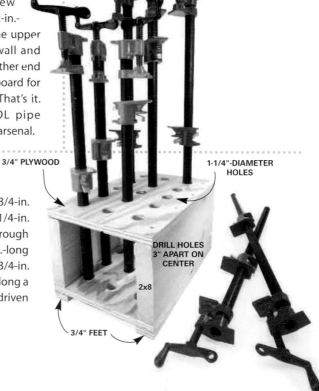

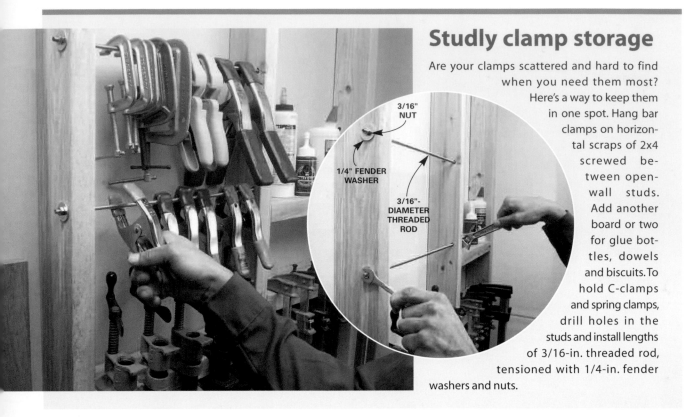

Studly clamp storage

Are your clamps scattered and hard to find when you need them most? Here's a way to keep them in one spot. Hang bar clamps on horizontal scraps of 2x4 screwed between open-wall studs. Add another board or two for glue bottles, dowels and biscuits. To hold C-clamps and spring clamps, drill holes in the studs and install lengths of 3/16-in. threaded rod, tensioned with 1/4-in. fender washers and nuts.

3/16" NUT

1/4" FENDER WASHER

3/16"-DIAMETER THREADED ROD

Keyhole pony clamp roost

You'll love this bar clamp rack because you can holster them securely without tightening the lower jaw against the rack. Just drop in the clamp and pull it out when needed. Notch the top piece of 1/2-in. plywood with the keyhole-shaped cutouts as shown, then screw it to the bottom piece of plywood. Make brackets from scrap wood and screw the rack to the wall.

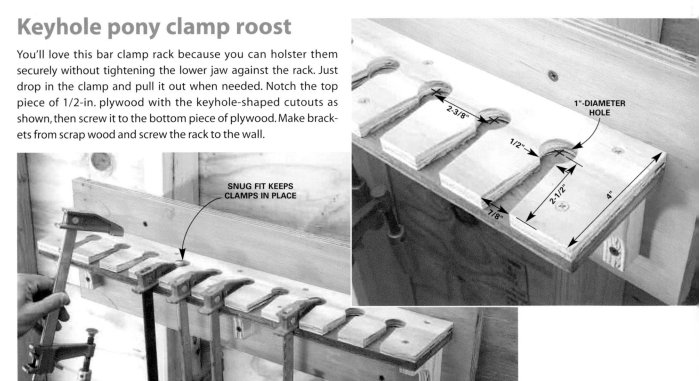

SNUG FIT KEEPS CLAMPS IN PLACE

2-3/8"

1/2"

1"-DIAMETER HOLE

2-1/2"

7/8"

4"

1

EYE BOLT

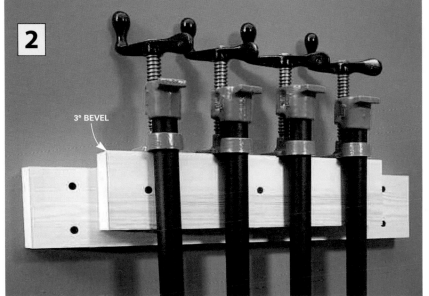

2

3° BEVEL

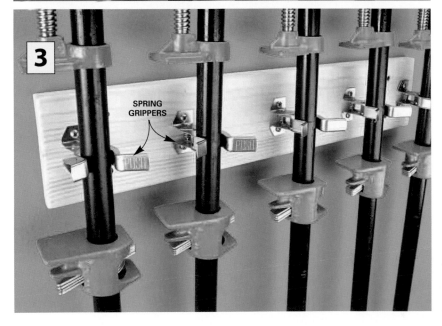

3

SPRING
GRIPPERS

Three pipe clamp storage ideas

You can never have enough clamps around the shop. Where to store them is another matter, however. Here are three simple ideas:

1. Buy screw-on pipe caps to fit the diameter of the pipe, then drill a small hole, attach an eye bolt and nuts and screw on the cap. Then hang them from a hook or nail.

2. Or make a simple rack out of scrap wood. Cut the top edge at a 3-degree bevel to keep the pipe clamps from slipping off the rack.

3. Or buy these spring grip organizers, available at home centers, then screw them to a board. Position the board just high enough to hold the pipe near the crank end while the other end rests on the floor.

Spring clamp roost

Keep your spring clamps springy for a lifetime! Don't store them clamped on a board; the springs will lose their tension. Instead, keep them on a metal towel rod ($3 at a home center). With the towel rod roost, you'll always know where to find these useful clamps in the heat of production.

SPRING CLAMPS

CHEAP TOWEL
RACK

Tips for storing hardware

PLYWOOD TRAY REST

1/2" PLYWOOD TOTE

ADD LABELS HERE IF YOU WISH

Muffin tin storage bin

Rescue those blackened, neglected muffin tins from a dark cupboard corner and put them to work holding small fasteners, nails, eyescrews, washers, electrical parts and more. Screw together a tote from three pieces of 1/2-in.-thick plywood cut to fit the width and height of your trays. Screw plywood strips on the inside to act as drawer runners for the tins, and glue or screw on a thin plywood back. The tote shown here holds four tins, but you can build it higher for even more storage capacity. Cut the plywood sides long enough so there's room to add a 3/4-in.-diameter dowel handle.

Rust-free nail storage

For rust-free storage of expensive air-nailer fasteners, use steel ammunition boxes from an army surplus store. They have a watertight seal to help prevent corrosion and they're cheap (about $5).

NAIL GUN AMMO CASE

Easy-to-read nail sizes

Here's a better and more permanent labeling method for coffee cans. Spray a stripe of white appliance paint across the outside face of each coffee can. When it dries, write the nail specs on the paint with a permanent marker. Appliance paint has a tough, gloss finish so it doesn't chip easily.

Adjustable bins

Nail down the hardware organization in your shop. Build these bin racks with removable partitions to suit the size of the hardware you're storing. For one rack, you'll need:

- One 3/8-in. x 24-in. x 7-1/8-in. plywood piece for the sides
- One 3/8-in. x 24-in. x 4-3/4-in. plywood piece for the floor
- Two 1/2-in. x 4-1/2-in. x 4-in. plywood pieces for the ends
- Five 1/8-in. x 4-1/2-in. x 4-3/8-in. hardboard partitions

On a table saw, cut 3/16-in.-deep slots every 4 in. across the 24-in. x 7-1/8-in. piece of plywood. Make the slots just wide enough for the 1/8-in.-thick partition to slide in smoothly. Now saw the slotted piece into strips 4-1/2 in. and 2-1/2 in. wide. Use 1-in. brads and glue (predrilling for the brads) to assemble the sides and angled ends, then nail and glue on the floor. Drop the angled partitions into the slots, mount the rack to a wall, and go nuts sorting and organizing your scattered hardware.

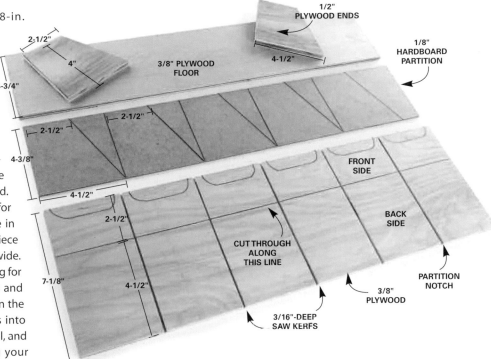

Nuts and washers stored on pegboard

Old-fashioned shower curtain rings ($2 for a 12-pack at a home center) can organize and conveniently display nuts and washers on your pegboard. Load up the rings, add a tape label and hang them near the wrenches. You can also toss them in a nail apron for on-the-go repairs.

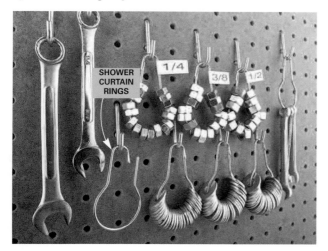

SHOWER CURTAIN RINGS

1/4   3/8   1/2

Recycled peanut-butter jars

Plastic peanut-butter jars work better for storage than glass baby food jars because they hold a lot more hardware and won't smash into slivers if you drop one. Attach the lids of 28-oz. jars under a shelf with two screws (so the lid can't spin when you loosen the jar) and screw on the loaded jar. For quick access, cut away half of a 64-oz. peanut-butter jar with a sharp utility knife, leaving the neck intact, then attach the lid and jar to the side of a cabinet.

TRIM WITH UTILITY KNIFE

64-OZ. JAR

ATTACH LID WITH TWO SCREWS

28-OZ. JAR

Magnetic mini storage

Want a handy storage roost for all the little screws, earplugs, nuts and washers in your shop? Pick up a package of Glad 4-oz. cups, a magnetic strip, several 7/16-in. washers and a tube of E6000 glue ($4 at craft and hobby stores). Apply glue to the cup's concave bottom, press in a washer flush with the bottom rim and let the glue set for 24 hours. Mount the magnet, load the cups, snap on the lids and all your itty-bitties are easy to spot, nab and put away. Magnetic tool-holder strips are available from Rockler (800-279-4441, rockler.com) and Magnaproducts (800-338-0527, shop-mag.com).

The magnetic strip provides more than enough magnet power to hold a cup crammed with screws.

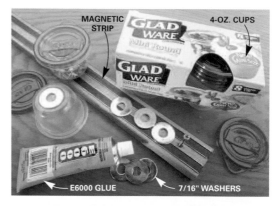

MAGNETIC STRIP   4-OZ. CUPS

GLAD WARE Mini Round

E6000 GLUE   7/16" WASHERS

SEE-THROUGH SIDES

WIDE MOUTH FOR EASY GRABBING

Recycled oil bottles I

Save up 12 plastic oil quart bottles, cut away one side with a utility knife, scrub out the oil residue and load them with nails and screws. Build a carrying case from scrap 1/2-in. and 1/4-in. plywood. Then label the bottle caps and slide in the bottles. Add a handle and tote it to your next project.

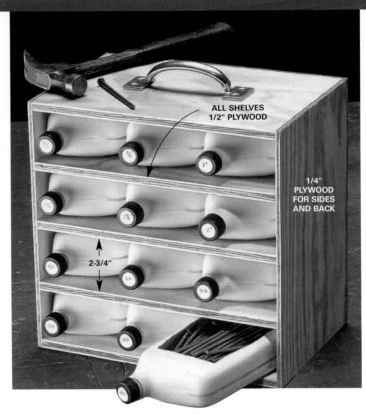

ALL SHELVES
1/2" PLYWOOD

1/4"
PLYWOOD
FOR SIDES
AND BACK

2-3/4"

CUT WINDOW
WITH UTILITY
KNIFE

ADHESIVE
LABEL

Recycled oil bottles II

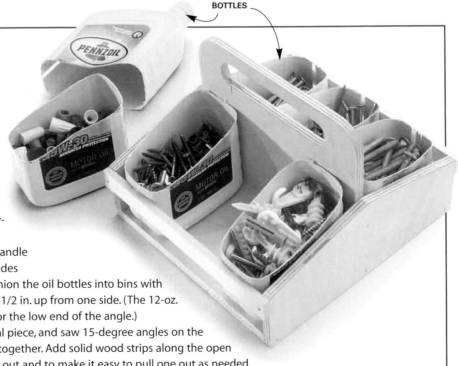

PLASTIC OIL
BOTTLES

Here's a fun project to keep your screws, nails, nuts and electrical whatsits handy and neatly organized. To make one, you'll need:

- Six quart-size motor oil bottles (empty!)
- One 9-in. x 7-3/4-in. floor made from 3/8-in. or 1/2-in. plywood
- One 7-3/4-in. x 6-in. plywood handle
- Two 3-1/2-in. x 9-in. plywood sides

With a utility knife or snips, fashion the oil bottles into bins with 15-degree angled sides starting 2-1/2 in. up from one side. (The 12-oz. hash mark on the bottle is great for the low end of the angle.)

Saw a handle slot in the vertical piece, and saw 15-degree angles on the sidepieces. Glue and nail the tote together. Add solid wood strips along the open sides to keep the bins from falling out and to make it easy to pull one out as needed.

Screw carousel

Build this spinning screw organizer and dial up the right fastener and tool with a touch of your fingers.

Trace the disc shapes onto the plywood using a compass and cut them out with a jigsaw or band saw. Sand the edges and drill holes in the center of each disc with a 1-in.-diameter spade bit. Also drill several 3/8-in. holes around the rim of the 4-in. disc for screwdrivers, and a few stopped 1/4-in.-diameter holes for driver bits.

Secure five containers to the 11-in. disc with 1/2-in. screws, using two screws to anchor each container.

Here's what you'll need to build it:

- One 11-in.-diameter x 3/4-in. plywood disc
- One 4-in.-diameter x 3/4-in. plywood disc
- One 11-in. x 1-in.-diameter dowel
- One 4-in. low-profile lazy Susan ($2.69 at rockler.com; part No. 28969)
- One 2-in.-diameter wood wheel
- One package of Ziploc 8-oz. Snap 'n Seal food containers

Glue the dowel in the 11-in. disc, then run a bead of glue around the dowel 4 or 5 in. up from the bottom and glue on the 4-in. disc, sliding it down from the top. When the glue is dry, screw the lazy Susan under the base with 1/2-in. screws and the wood wheel on top of the dowel. Load it with screws and give it a whirl!

P.S. Add stick-on labels to the lids.

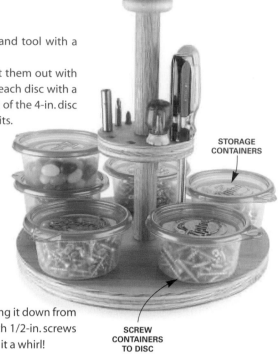

STORAGE CONTAINERS

SCREW CONTAINERS TO DISC

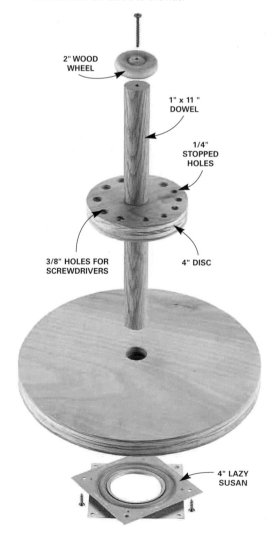

2" WOOD WHEEL

1" x 11" DOWEL

1/4" STOPPED HOLES

3/8" HOLES FOR SCREWDRIVERS

4" DISC

4" LAZY SUSAN

Hardware lassos

To keep your hardware neat and accessible, thread nuts, washers, sockets and other items on short pieces of 12- or 14-gauge electrical wire, then hang them on a toolbox handle or a pegboard hook. Twist the ends of the wire into hook shapes that interlock for easy closing and opening.

12- OR 14-GAUGE INSULATED WIRE

Sweet, sweet hardware drawer

Put your breath mint addiction to good use! Keep your empty tins handy, and when you have a dozen or so, load them with hardware and place them in a custom-fit drawer. The drawer slides inside a frame that's enclosed on the sides and back. You can cut the wood with a jigsaw, but a table saw works best. Here's how to make it.

Cut the pieces in the cutting list, below. Tack and glue the drawer together with 1-in. brads, locating the sides and partition inside the front and back ends. Tack glides on the drawer's upper edges, and on the frame sides, then tack and glue the frame ceiling and back to the frame sides.

Install the frame for the drawer in a convenient spot, driving screws through the ceiling, then slide in the drawer.

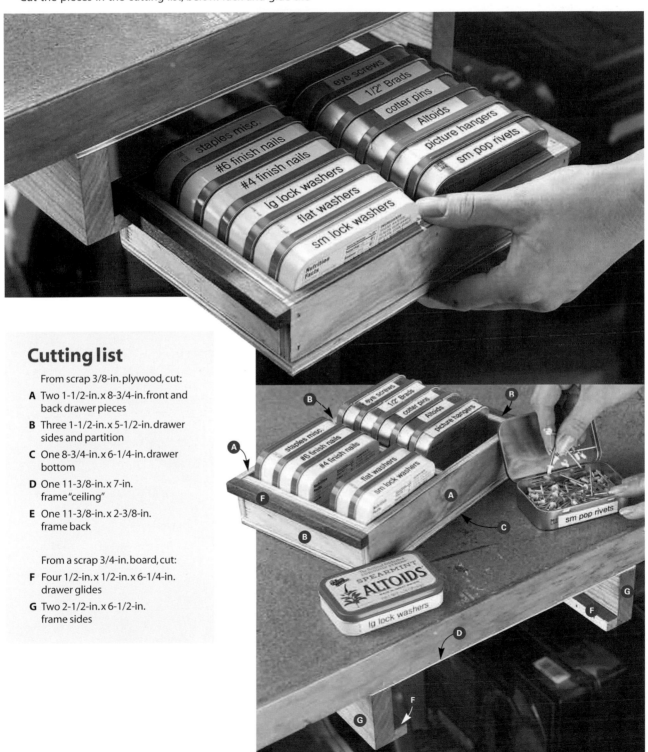

Cutting list

From scrap 3/8-in. plywood, cut:

A Two 1-1/2-in. x 8-3/4-in. front and back drawer pieces

B Three 1-1/2-in. x 5-1/2-in. drawer sides and partition

C One 8-3/4-in. x 6-1/4-in. drawer bottom

D One 11-3/8-in. x 7-in. frame "ceiling"

E One 11-3/8-in. x 2-3/8-in. frame back

From a scrap 3/4-in. board, cut:

F Four 1/2-in. x 1/2-in. x 6-1/4-in. drawer glides

G Two 2-1/2-in. x 6-1/2-in. frame sides

Hardware honeycomb

Finding the right fastener will be a snap with this multipocket storage bucket. To make one, round up a plastic 5-gallon bucket ($4 at a home center) and scrap plywood for partitions and floors. Use 3/4-in. plywood for the partitions and 1/4-in. plywood for the floors to match the bucket cutout dimensions shown.

Cut the bucket holes with a saber saw as shown, then saw the crisscrossing bottom partitions with slightly angled ends to fit snugly against the bucket sides. Saw notches halfway down the center of the partitions so they interlock. Next, cut the round floor to fit the bucket on top of the partition, then drop it in. Cut the next set of partitions, drop those in and then add the next floor. Create the egg carton partition to fit on top and screw or nail it to the upper floor. Then load your bucket. This system is designed for miscellaneous screws and nails; feel free to try your own configuration to fit your needs.

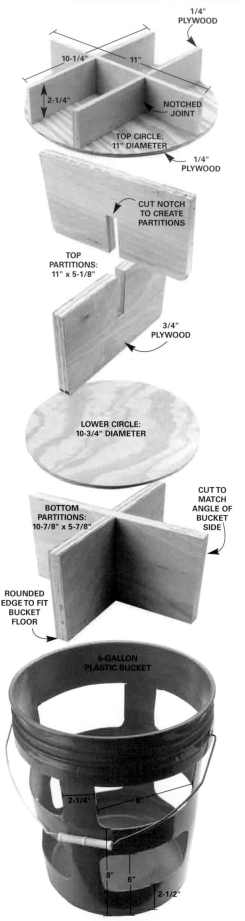

1/4" PLYWOOD

10-1/4"   11"

2-1/4"

NOTCHED JOINT

TOP CIRCLE: 11" DIAMETER

1/4" PLYWOOD

CUT NOTCH TO CREATE PARTITIONS

TOP PARTITIONS: 11" x 5-1/8"

3/4" PLYWOOD

LOWER CIRCLE: 10-3/4" DIAMETER

CUT TO MATCH ANGLE OF BUCKET SIDE

BOTTOM PARTITIONS: 10-7/8" x 5-7/8"

ROUNDED EDGE TO FIT BUCKET FLOOR

5-GALLON PLASTIC BUCKET

2-1/4"   6"

8"   6"

2-1/2"

Tidy fastener bins

Save those 100-oz. laundry detergent bottles and use them to hold jumbo supplies of screws and nails. Cut the top off the bottle (see right) to create a wide-mouth bin with a built-in handle. Label the bins, load them up, and you're ready to snag a handful when needed or carry a bin or two right to the job site.

TRACE AND CUT OUT

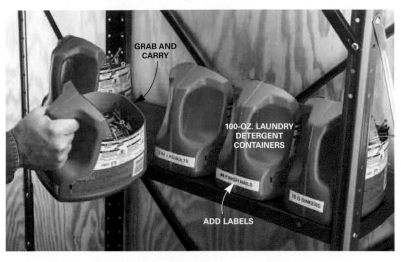

GRAB AND CARRY

100-OZ. LAUNDRY DETERGENT CONTAINERS

3 IN LAG BOLTS

#6 FINISH NAILS

10 D SINKERS

ADD LABELS

Super-cool hardware trays

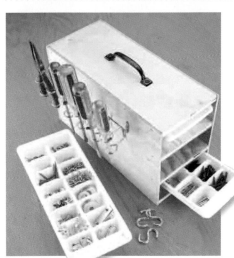

Forget the old coffee can filled with your lifetime collection of screws, washers and other hardware. Take 10 minutes to organize the miscellany in ice cube trays. Nail together a case from scrap plywood and carry it right to the job at hand.

Tasteful hardware storage

Save jumbo-sized Nesquik containers to hold nails, lag bolts and extra-long drywall screws up to 5 in. long. You can pack 4 lbs. of 16d nails in one can. They're great dispensers since the fasteners lie flat and are easy to grab, and they use space better than coffee cans when you store them on a shelf.

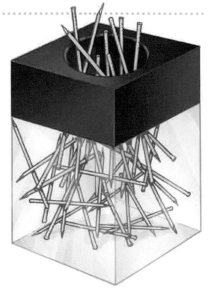

Nestlé Nesquik

5" NAILS OR OTHER STUFF

Nail dispenser

A great place to store finish nails, brads, screws and other small metal items is in those square plastic paper clip dispensers with the magnetic hole at the top. The items are easy to grab, and if you buy clear dispensers, you can see what's in them. And the contents are nearly impossible to spill.

Muffin tin hardware bins

Work surface cluttered with miscellaneous nails, screws, hardware, whatever? Clean it up and still keep that stuff at your fingertips.

Attach a muffin tin under a shelf with a single 1/4-in. x 1-1/2-in. flat head machine screw. The tin pivots out from beneath work surfaces to organize and serve up any little doodad you frequently use. And you store all that little stuff without using up a single square inch of workspace. For best results when installing your muffin bins:

■ Use muffin tins made from heavier gauge metal.

■ Drill and countersink a 1/4-in. hole in the shelf top, so the top of the screw is flush with the shelf.

■ Place 1/4-in. fender washers above and below the rim of the muffin tin.

■ Tighten two nuts against each other on the underside so the threads won't loosen.

PIVOT SCREW

FENDER WASHERS

FLAT HEAD MACHINE SCREW 1-1/2" x 1/4"

HEAVY-GAUGE MUFFIN TIN

Neat nail organizer

Bleach bottles make great nail organizers, once you cut out a section of the top. When the bottles are stored on their sides, the weight of the nails keeps them from rolling. The handles make for easy carrying, and they can stand upright when off the shelves.

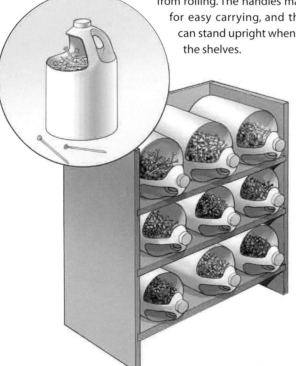

Soap box nail holder

Use a travel soap holder to store screws, nails and fasteners and protect them from rust. Tape the description from the original box onto the plastic container and you'll have all the information you need on a long-lasting package.

TRAVEL SOAP BOX

Clever storage solutions using PVC pipe

Additional ways to use PVC

- Snap-in caulk organizer, p. 56
- Caulk tube nest, p. 57
- Overhead storage, p. 64
- Odds-and-ends storage, p. 64
- Cordless drill holster, p. 69
- All-aboard shop vacuum, p. 70
- Vacuum attachment holder, p. 71
- Pipe clamp quivers, p. 72
- PVC pipe clamp rack, p. 73
- Cord holders, p. 102

Pipe clamp quivers, p. 72

Pegboard cubbyholes

To store slender tools and shop accessories, cut short lengths of PVC pipe (1-1/2- and 2-in.-diameter pipes work well for most items) and slide them over pegboard hooks. Then load them up with files, hacksaw blades, zip ties, pencils, stir sticks… you get the skinny.

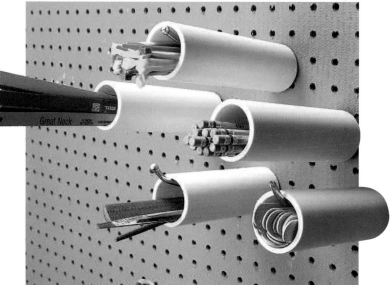

Panpipe tool storage

While this tool storage device may look like a variation on the Pan flute of Greek mythology, it's actually a great place to store tools that easily get lost—like chisels, files, pencils, scroll saw blades and hobby knives. For the fatter tools, use PVC cement to join short pieces of 1-1/4-in. PVC pipe side to side into a panpipe design, then add pieces of 1/2-in. pipe along the front of the flute for skinnier tools. Build a simple case around the pipes to create a floor and a back for hanging on a shop wall.

1/2" PVC PIPE

PVC tool pockets

You can holster your screwdrivers, chisels, files and other hand tools in 3-in.-long pieces of 1/2- and 3/4-in. PVC pipe. Cut away the upper open section with a hacksaw or band saw, drill a hole, screw the piece on a board, and drop in the tools. If you're using a band saw, slice off the cutaway section from a long length before cutting off the 3-in. holster.

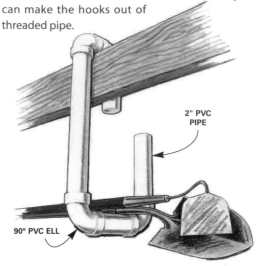

1" PVC

3/4" PVC

Custom storage hooks

Get ladders, tree pruners, bikes, 2x4s and other unwieldy items off your garage floor with these inexpensive PVC hooks. For heavier items, you can make the hooks out of threaded pipe.

2" PVC PIPE

90° PVC ELL

PVC holsters

Keep toothpicks, Q-Tips, Popsicle sticks, tongue depressors or other favorite gluing and finishing tools right at hand. Cut pieces of 2-in.-diameter PVC pipe at 10-degree angles and glue them to a board with Super Glue or construction adhesive. No more digging in drawers and dark shelf corners during the heat of project production!

10° ANGLE CUT

2"-DIAMETER PVC

PVC hammer holder

The next time you're out nailing, do it in style with this sturdy but stylish hammer holder. To make one, use a hacksaw or band saw to cut away one side of a 6-in.-long piece of 2-in. PVC pipe, leaving 2 in. at the bottom to drop the hammer inside it. To create belt slots, drill 1/4-in. holes in two lines and clean out the waste between the holes with a rat-tail file. That's it—drop in the hammer and enjoy its easy-to-reach location.

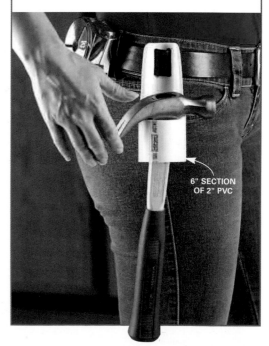

6" SECTION OF 2" PVC

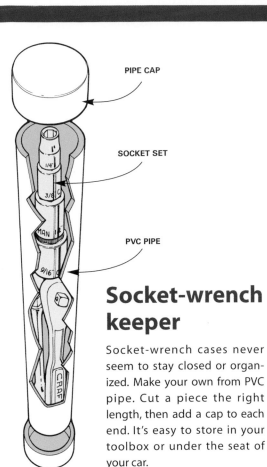

PIPE CAP

SOCKET SET

PVC PIPE

Socket-wrench keeper

Socket-wrench cases never seem to stay closed or organized. Make your own from PVC pipe. Cut a piece the right length, then add a cap to each end. It's easy to store in your toolbox or under the seat of your car.

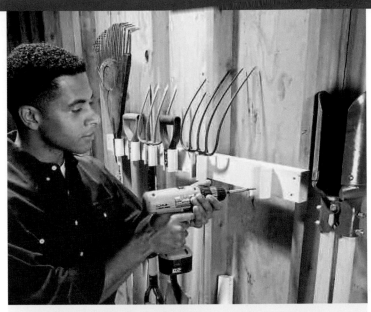

PVC tool holder

Build this PVC rack to store your tools on the wall. Use a jigsaw to cut a 1-1/4-in.-wide notch down the length of a 2-in.-diameter PVC pipe. Cut several 3-1/2-in.-long sections with a hacksaw or miter saw, and drill two 1/8-in. holes behind the notch. Use 1-1/4-in. drywall screws to attach these pieces to a 2x4 screwed to the wall.

PVC fastener trough and dowel quiver

For the fastener trough, cut a 2-ft. length of 4-in. PVC pipe lengthwise with a scroll saw, creating a trough that's a little more than half the pipe's diameter. Glue or screw in 1/2-in.-thick wood partitions to create compartments for often-used screw and nail sizes. To make it tip-proof,

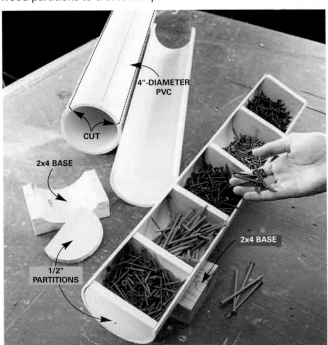

4"-DIAMETER PVC

CUT

2x4 BASE

1/2" PARTITIONS

2x4 BASE

trace the pipe's curve on a couple of scrap 2x4 blocks, power-sand or saw out the curve, and screw the pipe on this scrap block base.

For the dowel quiver, use a saber saw to cut lengthwise notches in a 30-in.-long piece of 3- or 4-in.-diameter pipe and then glue on a PVC end cap. Drill pilot holes in the pipe opposite the notches and screw the quiver to a shop wall. Your notched-out quiver will hold any size dowel—from standard 36-in. lengths to stubby leftovers—for instant access.

30"

PVC PIPE

PVC CAP

5"-LONG x 1-1/2"-DIAMETER PVC PIPE

3"-LONG x 3"-DIAMETER PVC PIPE

3" x 3" ANGLE BRACKET

2"-LONG x 3"-DIAMETER PVC PIPE

PVC socket shelves

Here's a great way to use leftover pieces of PVC pipe. Cut them into various shorter lengths and glue them to a 4-in.-wide board with construction adhesive. Attach the boards to a shop wall with angle brackets ($3 for a four-pack at a home center) bent downward 15 degrees or so. Then fill the pipe pieces with screws, nails, glue, spray paint and, sure, a hot cup of coffee.

With the shelves angling a little downward, it's easier to see and grab the contents. Two-inch pieces of 3-in.-diameter pipe are great for screws and nails, and 5-in.-long pieces of 1-1/2-in.-diameter pipe are neat holsters for pencils, files, paintbrushes and Popsicle sticks.

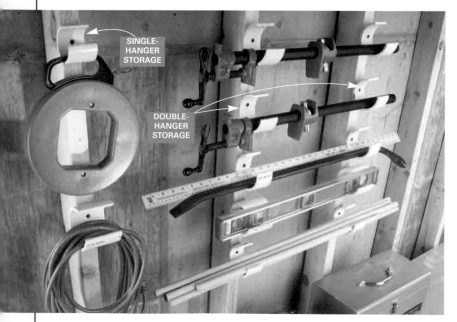

SINGLE-HANGER STORAGE

DOUBLE-HANGER STORAGE

PVC storage hangers

Cut 2-in. pieces of 3-in. PVC and saw away a 2-in. section so it looks like Pac-Man. (Remember Pac-Man?) Drill screw holes and attach the hangers to studs or shop walls. Space pairs for convenient horizontal storage of longer tools such as levels and glue clamps, and use single segments for ropes, electrical cords or anything else that you want securely stored yet easily accessible. Try this tip and you'll learn never to be peeved by leftover PVC.

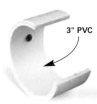

3" PVC

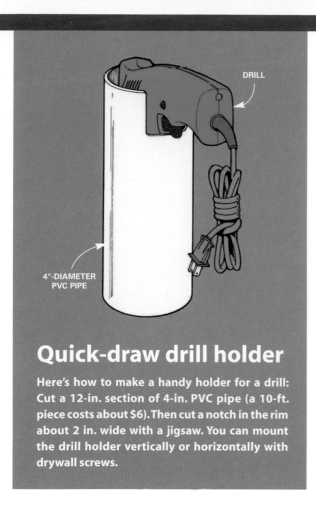

4"-DIAMETER
PVC PIPE

DRILL

Quick-draw drill holder

Here's how to make a handy holder for a drill: Cut a 12-in. section of 4-in. PVC pipe (a 10-ft. piece costs about $6). Then cut a notch in the rim about 2 in. wide with a jigsaw. You can mount the drill holder vertically or horizontally with drywall screws.

Cord organizer

Elastic cords can quickly become a tangled mess. Find the one you need at a glance with this handy rack made from 3- or 4-in. PVC pipe. Just drill 1/2-in.-diameter holes in the pipe to match the slightly stretched lengths of your cords. Keep it in your trunk or shop, out of the reach of children.

Quick-draw table saw accessories

Keep your table saw's miter gauge and push stick within ultra-easy reach with a couple of sections of 1-1/2-in. PVC pipe bolted or zip-tied to a convenient spot on the frame under the table. Attach the miter gauge holster using the existing frame bolts, or drill holes in the legs for machine screws. For the push stick holster, drill a couple of sets of matching holes about an inch apart on the pipe and tautly zip-tie it to the leg.

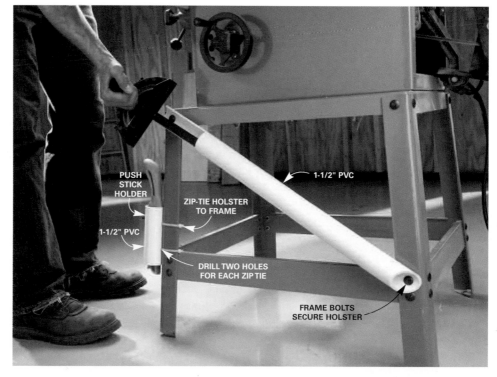

PUSH STICK HOLDER

1-1/2" PVC

ZIP-TIE HOLSTER TO FRAME

1-1/2" PVC

DRILL TWO HOLES FOR EACH ZIP TIE

FRAME BOLTS SECURE HOLSTER

Versatile pegboard

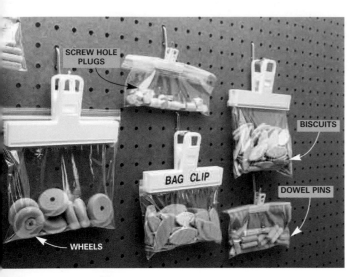

Bag-clip storage

Here's a great way to store dowel pins, biscuits, wood plugs and other wood project parts and keep them from swelling in the humidity. A few potato chip bag clips ($1 each at a grocery store) and zipper bags are all you need. Load, zip, clamp and hang them on pegboard to keep your mini wood items dry and easy to eye.

Secure pegboard hooks

Stop pegboard hooks from falling out when you remove the tools by squirting a dab of hot-melt glue in the pegboard hole before sticking the hook in. The glue remains pliable, so if you ever want to move the hook, just yank it out, scrape off the glue with a utility knife and glue the peg somewhere else.

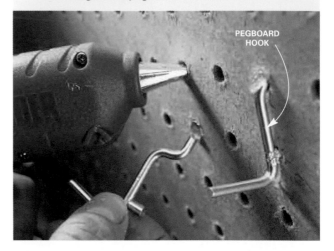

Pegboard shelves

Panel your shop with pegboard instead of drywall or plywood and there'll be no shortage of space to hang dozens of hand tools, no matter how small your shop is. Homemade shelving that's specifically for pegboard takes the concept one step further. Use 2x4s and 1/4-in. L-hooks to make the shelves. Bevel the top back edge so the shelf can be tipped in and tighten the L-hooks for a snug fit against the pegboard.

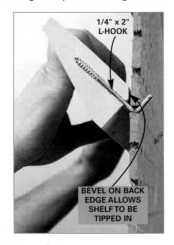

Predrill the edges of the 2x4s with a 3/16-in. drill bit and about every 6 in., screw in threaded 2-in. L-hooks to match the holes in your pegboard. These shelves are surprisingly strong and can be sized to fit your specific needs.

SLIDING DOORS

3/4" PLYWOOD TOP, BOTTOM AND SIDES

SLIDING DOOR HARDWARE

1/2" PLYWOOD SPACER

2" BETWEEN DOORS

FLOOR BRACKET

On-a-roll pegboard doors

Maximize hand tool storage in a tool cabinet. The key to this project is a 4-ft.-long By-Pass Sliding Door Hardware Set ($11 at a home center). You mount 1/4-in. pegboard onto it, making sure to provide enough room (2 in.) to hang tools on the pegboard and still allow it to slide by the door in front. The trick is to insert 1/2-in. plywood spacers in the roller hardware as shown. You can use the floor bracket that comes with the slider hardware to maintain the same 2-in. clearance at the bottom of the cabinet. For door handles, simply drill a couple of 1-1/4-in. holes in the pegboard with a spade bit. Now pop in the pegs and hang up your tools.

Pegboard shelves

Here's a slick way to store a whole cluster of tools on pegboard with only two pegs. Cut some 2-1/2-in.-wide mini shelves; drill holes or slots for router bits, screwdrivers, chisels and files; then drill a couple of 1/8-in. holes in the edges for the 1/8-in. diameter pegs. With a vise and pliers, bend the pegs to about 85 degrees and hammer them into the holes. Be sure the pegs fit tightly in the wood so the shelves can't fall off.

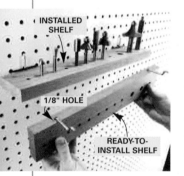

INSTALLED SHELF

1/8" HOLE

READY-TO-INSTALL SHELF

Corner-on pegboard hooks

Ever had a plane, level or square get dinged up after falling off the pegboard? Never again. Bend an 8-in.-long pegboard holder into a corner shape by holding it in a vise and pounding it with a hammer to make the series of right angles. Make one corner to hold the left side of the tool and another to hold the right. Now just hold the tool up to the pegboard and insert the corner peg so it clasps the tool's corner.

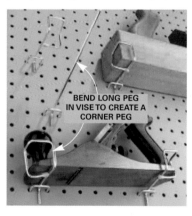

BEND LONG PEG IN VISE TO CREATE A CORNER PEG

Stud cavity storage

If your shop has a bare stud wall with plywood or OSB sheathing behind it, put it to work as a tool cabinet. To mount the back panel, glue 3/8-in. wood spacer strips to the sheathing. This will provide space to insert the pegs. Then screw 1/8-in. pegboard to the strips. Cut 1/4-in. pegboard doors and attach them to the studs with screws and butt or piano hinges, then add a latch. Now add pegs and load up the cabinet back and doors with tools.

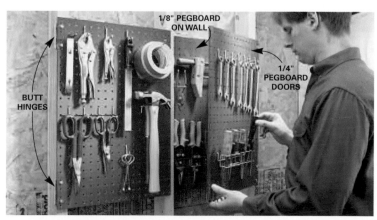

1/8" PEGBOARD ON WALL

1/4" PEGBOARD DOORS

BUTT HINGES

Pegboard tool-go-round

Build this handy rotating tool caddy with $35 for the wood at a home center and $15 for the hardware at a home center or Rockler Hardware, 800-279-4441, rockler.com.

With a table or circular saw, cut the pegboard strips (A). Cut the square pieces of 3/4-in. plywood (B) and nail two of them to the 1x4 boards (C) to make a stiff frame for the pegboard. Keep the boards toward the center as shown so they don't interfere with the pegboard holes.

Center and drill a 7/16-in. hole in the upper plywood square (B) and hammer in the tee nut from the top. Screw the machine screw through from the other side to create the pivot point.

Center and screw the bottom plywood square (B) to the top of the lazy Susan bearing and screw the third square under the bearing.

Nail or screw together the 3/4-in. plywood base from parts D and E, then nail or screw the third plywood square (B) on top of the base to join the spinning frame to the base. Screw the 10-in. pegboard strips to the frame.

Drill a 1/2-in. hole in one end of the steel bar for the upper pivot bushing, then bend the bar to create a 10-in. space between the pivot point and the wall. Drill holes for screws in the other end of the bar, slide the brass bushing onto the machine screw, slide on the bar and attach the other end of the bar to the wall.

9" LAZY SUSAN BEARING

Pivot Detail

3/8" NUT

3/8" BRASS BUSHING

3/8" TEE NUT

2-1/2" MACHINE SCREW

Materials list

2 2' x 4' x 1/4" pegboard sheets
2 1x4 x 4' pine boards
1 2' x 4' x 3/4" plywood
1 9" round lazy Susan (rockler.com, part No. 18531, $6)
1 3/8" tee nut
1 3/8" x 2-1/2" machine screw
1 3/8" brass bushing
1 3/8" tee nut
1 16" length of 1" x 1/8" flat steel bar

Cutting list

KEY	PCS.	SIZE & DESCRIPTION
A	4	1/4" x 10" x 48" pegboard
B	3	3/4" x 10" x 10" plywood
C	2	3/4" x 3-1/2" x 46-1/2" pine boards
D	2	3/4" x 10" x 20" plywood
E	2	3/4" x 8-1/2" x 20" plywood

Toolboxes, carriers and organizers for hand tools

Roll-around tool caddy

This simple workstation rolls right up to the job—anywhere in your work area. With your specialty tools organized and at your fingertips,

you can concentrate on the project at hand. No more wandering around the shop gathering your materials.

The caddy shown here is configured for woodturning and ready to roll up to the lathe. If you're a gearhead, you could build it with a flat top with bins for sockets and wrenches, and shelves below for car supplies. If you're a woodworker, outfit it with planes, mallets and chisels. Whatever you use it for, when you're done for the day, you can just roll it out of the way.

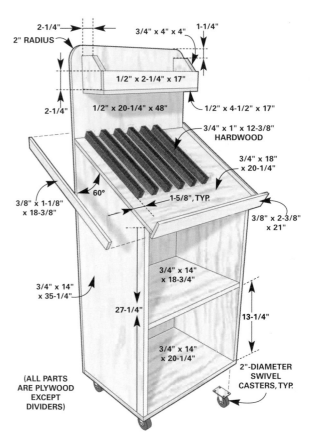

2-1/4"
2" RADIUS
3/4" x 4" x 4"
1-1/4"
1/2" x 2-1/4" x 17"
2-1/4"
1/2" x 20-1/4" x 48"
1/2" x 4-1/2" x 17"
3/4" x 1" x 12-3/8" HARDWOOD
3/4" x 18" x 20-1/4"
3/8" x 1-1/8" x 18-3/8"
60°
1-5/8", TYP.
3/8" x 2-3/8" x 21"
3/4" x 14" x 35-1/4"
3/4" x 14" x 18-3/4"
27-1/4"
13-1/4"
3/4" x 14" x 20-1/4"
2"-DIAMETER SWIVEL CASTERS, TYP.

(ALL PARTS ARE PLYWOOD EXCEPT DIVIDERS)

Vinyl gutter tool tray

What can you do with a leftover length of gutter? You can screw it to the edge of your workbench

and use it to keep tools and fasteners out of your way but still handy for assembly work.

Elastic-cord tool holder

Use elastic cords to make a portable tool organizer for chisels and other hand tools. Fasten one end of the cord to a 1x8 with an electrical staple, lay the cord straight without stretching it, then staple the other end. Add staples every 3 in. to create holders, leaving the staples just loose enough so the cord can still move. Then fasten the 1x8 to the wall.

ELASTIC CORD

3" DOOR HINGE

2x4

PLYWOOD BLOCK

Tool storage book

Hang 1/2- or 3/4-in.-thick plywood "pages" 4 in. apart on horizontal 2x4s with 3-in. door hinges. Screw and glue 3/4-in. plywood blocks between the hinges and the 2x4s so the pages can pivot without binding. The pages shown are 16 in. wide x 24 in. long, but you can build them whatever size you need.

CARPET SCRAP

Tidier tool trays

A piece of short-pile carpet in the bottom of each tray in your tool chest will keep tools from shifting and knocking about. So the next time you open the tray, the tools will still be laid out nice and neat the way you left them. Another benefit: less noise.

Pointy-tool pincushion

Here's a handy way to store pointed tools for instant availability. Drill 5/8-in. holes through a few 4- or 5-in. foam craft balls ($3 each at a craft store), and skewer and glue them along a 5/8-in.-diameter dowel with construction adhesive. Screw together a 3/4-in. wood bracket, drilling a stopped 5/8-in.-diameter hole 1/2 in. deep in the bottom end and a 3/4-in. hole through the upper end. Screw the bracket at a convenient height, slide in the foam balls and load them with drill, router and spade bits; paintbrushes; screwdrivers; Allen wrenches; awls; X-Acto knives; pencils and, well, you get the point.

FOAM BALLS

PIVOT

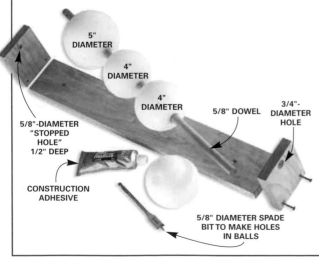

5" DIAMETER

4" DIAMETER

4" DIAMETER

5/8" DOWEL

3/4"- DIAMETER HOLE

5/8"-DIAMETER "STOPPED HOLE" 1/2" DEEP

CONSTRUCTION ADHESIVE

5/8" DIAMETER SPADE BIT TO MAKE HOLES IN BALLS

Double-decker tote

This handy double-decker carryall is great for toting tools and hardware to the job site. Build it from a quarter sheet of 3/4-in. plywood, 1/8-in. hardboard strips, glue, nails and a 1-1/4-in. dowel. Cut the pieces as shown; just keep in mind that it works best to cut the 3/8-in.-deep slots for the hardboard dividers before you cut the sides away from the base. An average 1/8-in. kerf saw blade in your table saw works perfectly for cutting the 1/8-in. hardboard dividers. Be sure to cut the dado "key" slots (using multiple passes with your table saw) in the ends of the top tray to lock it to the tote tabs so you can carry it as a unit. Make these slots about 1/16 in. wider than the 3/4-in. x 3/8-in. tabs so you don't have to struggle to lift the top tray off the bottom tray.

All pieces 3/4" plywood unless otherwise noted

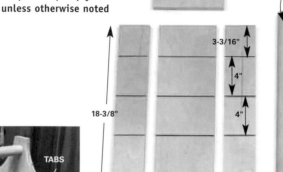

1/4" HOLE
3/8" DEEP

1-1/4" DOWEL

11"

7"

7"

3-3/16"

4"

4"

4"

18-3/8"

20-3/4"

4"

20"

3-3/16"

5-1/2"

3"

4"

5-1/2"

3"

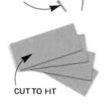

1/8" HARD-BOARD

NO. 8 x 1-1/4" SCREWS

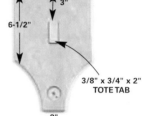

CUT TO FIT

3"

6-1/2"

3/8" x 3/4" x 2" TOTE TAB

2"

TABS

KEY SLOT

Hijacked tackle box

When the fishing urge stops biting, put that old tackle box to use as a portable hardware and tool tote. Load the nifty fold-out compartments with screws, nails, bolts, tape, electrical connectors —what have you. Stash your pliers, screwdriver, wrenches, hammer, tape measure and other frequently used tools on the bottom level. When chores and repairs start nibbling at your conscience, you'll have the right tackle handy for the job.

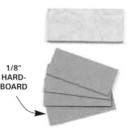

MOBILE HARDWARE AND TOOLS

Instant tool holder

Store chisels, files, large drill bits, screwdrivers and other long tools so they're both visible and close at hand. Simply cut off the top from a clear 2-liter plastic soft drink bottle, leaving a flap for hanging. Use smaller bottles for smaller tools.

Vertical storage

Hardware cloth tool roost

Store just about every hand tool you need on a strip of vinyl-coated 1/2-in. wire mesh hardware cloth. Make a frame from a scrap of plywood and a couple of 5-in.-long 2x4s. Span the 2x4s with the mesh and staple it on, then bend over the front of the mesh to cover the 2x4 ends. Now have fun filling the mesh with any tool that has a shaft that'll fit through the holes. Or for chisels, pliers and larger-handled tools, just snip out wider openings in the mesh with a wire cutter. For a wrench roost, snip and bend up wires along the front edge of the mesh to make little hanging hooks.

Chisel pockets

Here's a neat tabletop chisel storage idea that's a snap to build from scrap boards. It angles the handles toward you for easy reach.

Start with a 4-in.-wide board. Using your table saw, cut stopped slots to match the width and depth of each chisel (plus some wiggle room). Screw or glue on another board to create the pockets, then run the lower edge of the doubled board through a table saw with the blade set at 15 degrees. Now cut three triangular legs with 75-degree bottom corners and glue them to the pocket board.

If you like, drill a few holes through the boards for pegboard hooks so the holder is easy to store on the wall.

75°

VARIED WIDTH SLOTS FOR CHISELS

3-1/2" TO 4"

Pointy tool tray

Here is a cool way to keep screwdrivers and all other pointy tools at hand. Drill a grid of holes in a 10 x 20-in. piece of plywood, leaving room on the ends for handle slots. To create the ends of the slots, drill 1-1/4-in. holes with a spade bit. Then connect the holes with parallel lines and saw out the slots with a saber or keyhole saw. Make or buy some short legs, screw them on and serve up your tools!

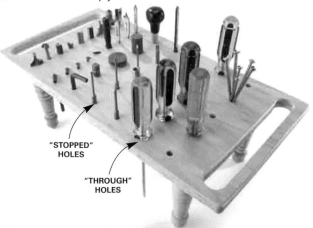

"STOPPED" HOLES

"THROUGH" HOLES

New angle on small-tool storage

Find a bare spot on a wall or workbench and screw on a 2-ft. piece of 2-in.-wide, slotted-angle iron available at home centers. It's the perfect hangout for screwdrivers, bits, safety glasses and sanding drums.

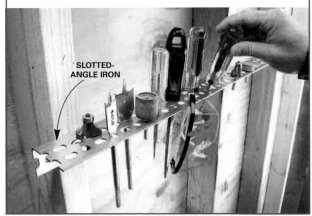

SLOTTED-ANGLE IRON

Stationary "tool belt"

What do you do with your old belts now that you've changed your waistline to a larger or smaller size? Mount one to the front of a shelf in your workshop with screws and finish washers. Just pucker enough of the belt to hold the tool you need and drive in a screw. Move your way along the shelf until your favorite tools are handily in place.

Angle-iron tool slots

Screw a length of leftover slotted angle to the side of your workbench to keep tools at hand. The slots work especially well for screwdrivers and wrenches.

1-1/2" x 1-1/2" ANGLE

Wrenches

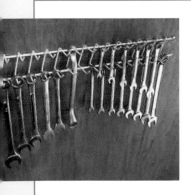

A wrench rack from the clothes closet

Are all your wrenches stuffed in a plastic bucket? Here's a better idea: Screw a tie/belt rack (available at discount stores) to a bare spot on the wall over your workbench and hang the wrenches—SAE and metric—where you can swiftly nab and put them away in an orderly fashion.

ROUTER COLLET WRENCHES

LIGHT CHAIN

SPLIT KEY RING

A chain gang of router wrenches

Ever been here, done this? A Saturday afternoon's worth of woodworking creates a pile of tools, bottles, boards, clamps and chips on your workbench. You need a new bit in the router, but a search produces only one collet wrench. Thirty minutes later, you unbury the second wrench.

To avoid bit-changing rage, use this simple tip: Buy a pair of small split key rings and a short length of small-gauge chain, and shackle the wandering wrenches into a single, easy-to-hang, hard-to-lose unit. You'll enjoy bit-changing serenity forever.

Wrenches bound in the round

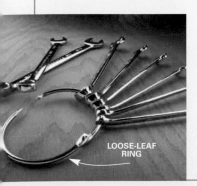

LOOSE-LEAF RING

You need a 5/8-in. wrench but can't find it in the drawer without rummaging around and eyeballing all the other scattered wrenches. Instead, store your end wrenches on a 3-1/2-in.-diameter loose-leaf ring ($1 at a hardware store). It only takes a second to snap the ring open and pull off the one you need. And you can throw them back into the toolbox knowing they'll stay together next time.

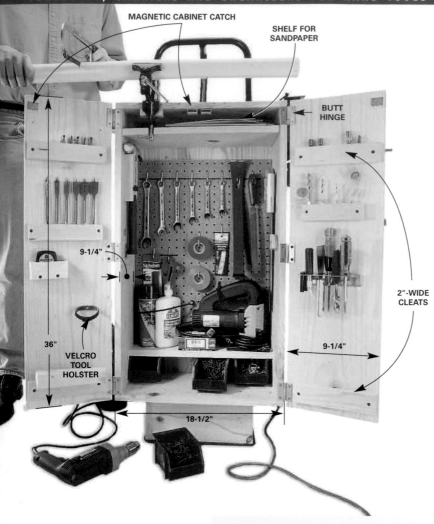

MAGNETIC CABINET CATCH

SHELF FOR SANDPAPER

BUTT HINGE

2"-WIDE CLEATS

9-1/4"

9-1/4"

36"

VELCRO TOOL HOLSTER

18-1/2"

Mobile tool chest

Build this mobile tool chest and take all your tools to the job in just one trip. A new dolly costs about $35 and the boards for the cabinet about $20. If you use 1x10 pine boards, you won't need to cut any boards to width.

Screw the cabinet together with 1-5/8-in. drywall screws after drilling pilot holes. Clamp on the plywood back, check for square, then screw it to the sides, top and floor with 1-in. drywall screws. Attach the doors with 2-1/2-in. butt hinges.

Pine boards tend to warp, so to keep the doors flat, screw several 2-in.-wide cleats across the inside. The cleats can be drilled to double as great drill and driver bit holders.

To raise the cabinet to a more comfortable height, screw four scrap boards into a frame and attach this base to the dolly's base with lag screws. Next drill holes in the base, then rest the cabinet on the base and attach it with 1-5/8-in. drywall screws through the floor into the base. To attach the upper part of the cabinet to the dolly, drive two 5/16-in.-diameter bolts through a board positioned behind the dolly's frame and into two 5/16-in. tee nuts set in the cabinet back. If this won't work for your dolly or design, use metal strapping or drill a couple of bolt holes through the dolly.

The cabinet's 9-1/4 in. depth provides plenty of space for power and hand tools plus full sheets of sandpaper. Have fun engineering convenient holders for your tools using pegboard, magnets, hooks and shop-fashioned holsters. Be sure to securely store tools so they won't fall or roll around as you cruise to and from the job.

Materials list

- 4 36-in.-long 1x10 pine boards (actually 3/4 in. x 9-1/4 in.) for the doors and sides
- 2 18-1/2-in.-long 1x10 pine boards for the cabinet top and floor
- 1 18-1/2-in. x 36-in. piece of 1/2-in.-thick plywood for the back

  Scrap boards for a base

  Assorted fasteners

BARREL BOLT LATCH

BASE

EXTENSION CORD ABOARD

ATTACH CABINET TO DOLLY WITH 5/16" BOLTS

MOUNTING BOARD

Controlling cords & wires

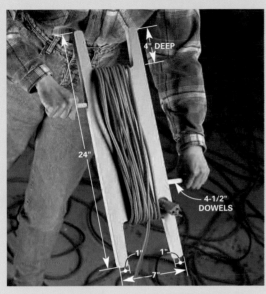

Quick-wind cord holder

Tired of untangling those long extension cords every time you need one? Cut notches in the ends of a scrap board, glue in a couple 1/2-in.-diameter dowel handles and reel in every cord in your shop. There's enough room for 150 ft. of medium-duty (14-gauge) cord if you cut the holder the same size as the one shown.

Sawhorse hook

Extend the top on your sawhorses and screw in a large hook (sold for hanging bicycles). It's handy for keeping an extension cord out from underfoot, or you can hang your circular saw on it instead of putting the saw on a dusty floor.

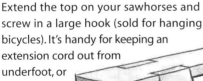
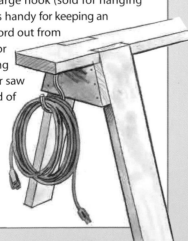

Bucket-lid cord reel

Make this handy cord reel using extra bucket lids from drywall mud pails. Cut a 5-in. length of 4x4 and then cut a groove in the side the same width as your cord. Fasten the lids to the 4x4 with 1/4 x 2-in. lag screws. Make handles from an old 1-1/8-in.-diameter broom handle and drill a 1/2-in. hole through the center. Fasten the crank to the lid with bolts, nuts and washers, and apply Loctite sealant to the end nut. Fasten the handle to the 4x4 through the lid with a 6-1/2-in. lag screw. Just insert your cord and reel it in.

6-1/2" LAG SCREW AND WASHER

END NUT

4" WOOD HANDLE

1/2" x 5" BOLT WITH NUTS ON EACH SIDE

Hook-and-chain cord hanger

A length of chain and a wall-mounted coat hook provide a secure hangout for bulky electrical cords or other cumbersome coils. Hang one end of the chain on the lower hook, then loop the chain around the coiled cord and attach the other end of the chain to the upper hook.

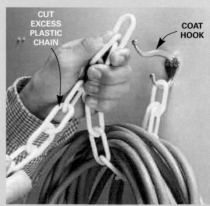

CUT EXCESS PLASTIC CHAIN

COAT HOOK

Extension cord coil keepers

Here are three easy ways to keep cords tightly coiled, even when they fall off the hook or get shoved into a toolbox:

■ Velcro strips. Buy a pack of 10 precut, preslotted strips ($2 at a home center) or pick up a roll of hook-and-loop material at a fabric store and make your own.

■ 3/8-in.-diameter rope. Attach to the end of the cord as shown, then tie up the coiled cord.

■ Elastic ponytail holders that secure with plastic balls on the ends work great on coiled extension cords too.

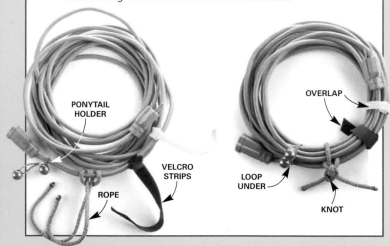

PONYTAIL HOLDER

ROPE

VELCRO STRIPS

OVERLAP

LOOP UNDER

KNOT

CLEAR TUBING

SPEAKER WIRE

Cord holder

Here's a good way to tidy up lamp cords or speaker wires and keep them up off the floor. Slit short lengths of clear plastic tubing and fasten them to your baseboard with a staple or tack.

Cleaning up wires

Before you ditch that old phone, cut off the coiled handset cord. You can wrap it around the tangle of wires behind your stereo or computer to keep it organized.

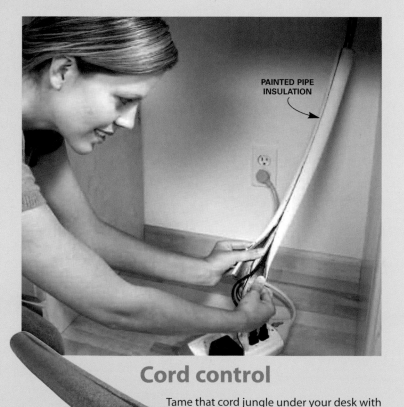

PAINTED PIPE INSULATION

Cord control

Tame that cord jungle under your desk with a length of 1/2-in. foam pipe insulation. Paint it the color of your wall and it will virtually disappear.

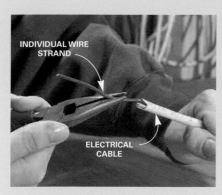

INDIVIDUAL WIRE STRAND

ELECTRICAL CABLE

HANGING HOOK

WRAPPED AROUND CORD

Cord keeper

Individual strands of electrical cable make great cord and hose wraps. Cut 12- or 14-gauge electrical cable into 12-in. to 18-in. sections. Grip a single strand with a needle-nose pliers, hold the casing and pull out the individual strand. It's easy to wrap and unwrap the wire around cords or hoses. Twist a loop on the opposite end of the wire for hanging.

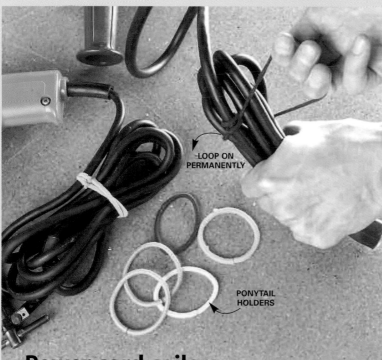

LOOP ON PERMANENTLY

PONYTAIL HOLDERS

Power cord coilers

Got a shelf loaded with drills, saws, sanders and routers but can't untangle the cords to safely pull one off the shelf? Try this: Buy a pack of elastic ponytail holders ($2) and use them to keep the cords neatly coiled while the tools are stored. Snugly loop the ponytail holder around the cord so it stays on the cord while you're using the tool.

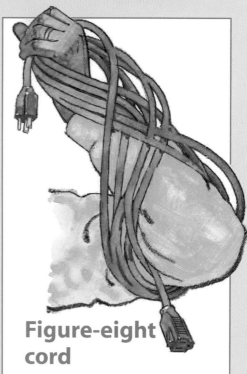

Figure-eight cord

Lots of people use the "elbow and thumb" method for winding up an extension cord. An improvement is to wind the cord with a figure-eight motion. Your coil will easily unwind without tangling.

Tangle-free cord storage

To keep cords tangle-free, use a method called a "daisy chain," which entails creating a series of loops that feed through each other, yet come apart tangle-free. It can reduce a 50-ft. cord to a more manageable length of about 8 ft.

Start by folding the cord in half. Then hold the ends of the cord in your left hand, make an 8-in. loop (Photo 1) and reach through the loop with your right hand to grab the cord about a foot past the loop. Pull the 12 in. of cord through the first loop, creating another loop (Photos 2 and 3).

Make more loops, pulling a new loop through each preceding one until you reach the end of the cord (Photo 4). Then make a loose loop to keep the cord from coming unraveled and feed it through the last loop (Photo 5). To use the cord, unfasten the last loop and pull on the cord to straighten it out.

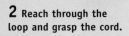

1 Fold the cord in half, then create a closed loop at one end.

2 Reach through the loop and grasp the cord.

3 Pull a section of cord back through the initial loop.

4 Continue making loops by pulling the cord through each newly created loop.

5 Make a final loop, then push it through the previous loop to hold it together.

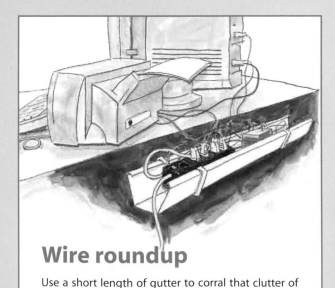

Wire roundup

Use a short length of gutter to corral that clutter of wires hanging down behind a computer desk or stereo cabinet. It keeps them off the floor.

Cord holders

You can temporarily hang extension cords on ceiling joists or along the edge of your workbench with these holders made of 1-in.-diameter PVC pipe. Cut a slot in a 6-in. piece of pipe, drill screw holes, then cut it into 1-in. lengths. A hacksaw for cutting the pipe, an electric drill and a vise are all the tools you need.

CHAPTER
4

Organize your **laundry room & closets**

On average, a family of four creates 10 loads of laundry per week. And once all those dirty clothes, towels and sheets are clean, there's got to be some place to put them!

An organized laundry area makes this ongoing chore more enjoyable and efficient. Plus shipshape closets make storing and finding your clothes, shoes, bedding and towels easier and much less frustrating. Here are our favorite simple, creative strategies for conquering clothing chaos.

Tips for tidy closets

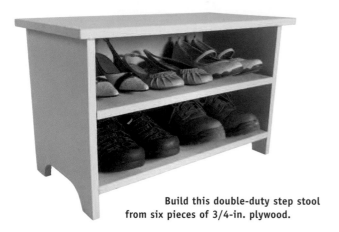

Build this double-duty step stool from six pieces of 3/4-in. plywood.

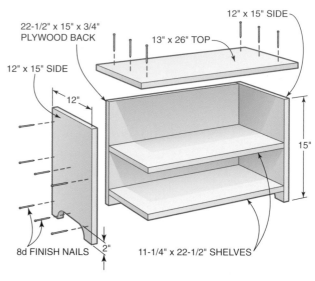

22-1/2" x 15" x 3/4" PLYWOOD BACK

12" x 15" SIDE

13" x 26" TOP

12" x 15" SIDE

12"

12" x 15" SIDE

15"

8d FINISH NAILS

2"

11-1/4" x 22-1/2" SHELVES

Shoe-storage booster stool

Build this handy stool in one hour and park it in your closet. You can also use it as a step to reach the high shelf. All you need is a 4 x 4-ft. sheet of 3/4-in. plywood, wood glue and a handful of 8d finish nails. Cut the plywood pieces according to the illustration. Spread wood glue on the joints, then nail them together with 8d finish nails. First, nail through the sides into the back. Then nail through the top into the sides and back. Finally, mark the location of the two shelves and nail through the sides into the shelves.

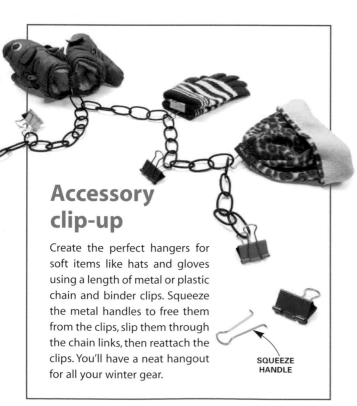

Accessory clip-up

Create the perfect hangers for soft items like hats and gloves using a length of metal or plastic chain and binder clips. Squeeze the metal handles to free them from the clips, slip them through the chain links, then reattach the clips. You'll have a neat hangout for all your winter gear.

SQUEEZE HANDLE

Trapeze clothes hanger

Here's a quick way to add another clothes rod in a closet. It's especially useful in a child's closet, because you can easily adjust the height to accommodate the changing wardrobe of a growing child. Use lightweight chain attached to both the upper and lower rods with screw hooks. Squeeze the screw hooks closed with pliers.

1-1/2" DOWEL

CHAIN

SCREW HOOK

Shoe ladder

Without constant vigilance, shoes tend to pile up into a mess next to entry doors. Untangle the mess with a simple, attractive shoe ladder that keeps everything from boots to slippers organized and off the floor.

Cut and drill the dowel supports (Photo 1), then screw them to 1x4s (Photo 2). Cut the 1x4s to fit your shoes and the available space—an average pair of adult shoes needs 10 in. of space. Nail or glue the dowels into the dowel supports, leaving 2 in. (or more) extending beyond the supports at the end to hang sandals or slippers.

Apply finish before you mount the shoe ladder to the wall. Screw the shoe ladder to studs or use heavy-duty toggle-bolt style anchors to hold it in place.

2 Predrill through the back of the 1x4 into the 1x3 supports, then glue and screw the pieces together.

Closet nook shelves

Salvage the hidden space at the recessed ends of your closets by adding a set of shelves. Wire shelves are available in a variety of widths. Measure the width and depth of the space. Then choose the correct shelving and ask the salesperson to cut the shelves to length for you or cut them yourself with a hacksaw. Subtract 3/8 in. from the actual width to determine the shelf length. Buy a pair of end mounting brackets and a pair of plastic clips for each shelf.

Two-story closet shelves

There's a lot of space above the shelf in most closets. Even though it's a little hard to reach, it's a great place to store seldom-used items. Make use of this wasted space by adding a second shelf above the existing one. Buy enough closet shelving material to match the length of the existing shelf plus enough for two end supports and middle supports over each bracket. Twelve-inch-wide shelving (about $9 for an 8-ft. length) is available in various lengths and finishes at home centers and lumberyards. These supports were cut at 16 in. long, but you can place the second shelf at whatever height you like. Screw the end supports to the walls at each end. Use drywall anchors if you can't hit a stud. Then mark the position of the middle supports onto the top and bottom shelves with a square and drill 5/32-in. clearance holes through the shelves. Drive 1-5/8-in. screws through the shelf into the supports.

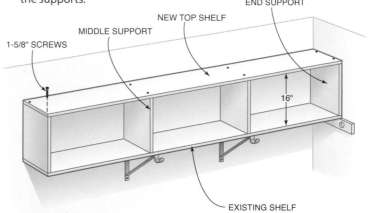

Glove and cap rack

Make a simple rack for gloves and caps on the back of your closet door. Straighten a coat hanger and feed it through the middle screw eye mounted to the door. Put as many clip clothespins on the wire as you need, then bend a loop in the wire at each end, around the outer screw eyes.

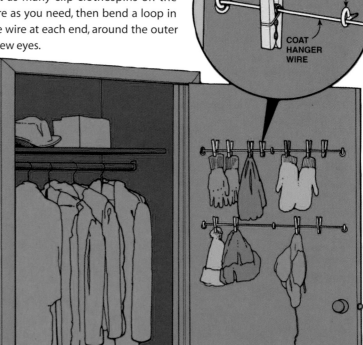

Double-duty luggage

Put your luggage to use when it's not on vacation. Fill it with off-season clothes and stash it under the bed.

Tie, scarf and belt organizer

Clean up a messy closet by hanging your ties, belts and scarves on this 3-in-1 closet organizer. All you need is a 2 x 2-ft. piece of 1/2-in. plywood ($10 to $15), a wooden hanger and a hook (the one shown was taken from a hanger).

This organizer is 12 in. wide and 16 in. tall, but yours can be taller or narrower. To get a nice curve at the top, use the wooden hanger as a guide. Center it, trace the edge and cut it out with a jigsaw. Make a pattern of holes, slots and notches on a piece of paper and transfer it to your board. Use a 2-in. hole saw to cut the holes, making sure the board is clamped down tightly to keep the veneer from chipping (Photo 1). Use a jigsaw to cut out the side notches. To cut the slots, punch out the ends with a 5/8-in. Forstner drill bit (or a sharp spade bit) to prevent chipping, and then use a jigsaw to finish cutting out the center of each slot (Photo 2).

Sand the wood and apply several coats of sealer or poly to smooth the edges so your scarves and ties don't snag (this is the most time-consuming step). Using a 1/4-in. round-over bit with a router makes the sanding go faster. Drill a small hole into the top of the organizer for your hook, squeeze in a bit of epoxy glue to hold it and then screw it in.

1 Drill scarf holes with a 2-in. hole saw. Clamp the plywood tightly against a piece of scrap wood to prevent chipping as the hole saw exits the plywood.

2 Use a 5/8-in. Forstner drill bit or a sharp spade bit to punch out the ends of the slots, and then finish cutting them out with a jigsaw.

Tips for a tidy laundry room

Closet rod and shelf

This project will save you hours of ironing and organizing. Now you can hang up your shirts and jackets as soon as they're out of the dryer—no more wrinkled shirts at the bottom of the basket. You'll also gain an out-of-the-way upper shelf to store all sorts of odds and ends.

Just go to your home center and get standard closet rod brackets, a closet rod and a precut 12-in.-deep melamine shelf (all for about $25). Also pick up some drywall anchors, or if you have concrete, some plastic anchors and a corresponding masonry bit. Follow the instructions in Photos 1 and 2.

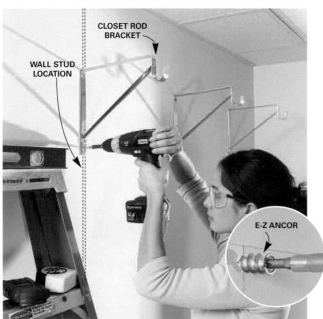

WALL STUD LOCATION

CLOSET ROD BRACKET

E-Z ANCOR

1 Draw a level line about 78 in. above the floor and locate the studs behind the drywall. Fasten at least two of your closet rod brackets into wall studs (4 ft. apart) and then center the middle bracket with two 2-in.-long screws into wall anchors (inset).

MELAMINE SHELF 3/4" x 12" x 72"

2 Fasten your 12-in.-deep melamine shelf onto the tops of the brackets with 1/2-in. screws. Next insert your closet rod, drill 1/8-in. holes into the rod, and secure it to the brackets with No. 6 x 1/2-in. sheet metal screws.

Behind-the-door shelves

The space behind a door is another storage spot that's often overlooked. Build a set of shallow shelves and mount it to the wall. The materials cost about $40. Measure the distance between the door hinge and the wall and subtract an inch. This is the maximum depth of the shelves. Use 1x4s for the sides, top and shelves. Screw the sides to the top. Then screw three 1x2 hanging strips to the sides: one top and bottom and one centered. Nail metal shelf standards to the sides. Complete the shelves by nailing a 1x2 trim piece to the sides and top. The 1x2 dresses up the shelf unit and keeps the shelves from falling off the shelf clips.

Locate the studs. Drill clearance holes and screw the shelves to the studs with 2-1/2-in. wood screws. Put a rubber bumper on the frame to protect the door.

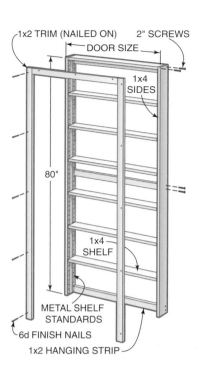

1x2 TRIM (NAILED ON)   2" SCREWS
DOOR SIZE
1x4 SIDES
80"
1x4 SHELF
METAL SHELF STANDARDS
6d FINISH NAILS
1x2 HANGING STRIP

Quick washer/dryer shelf

Clean up the clutter of detergent boxes, bleach bottles and other laundry room stuff. Install a shelf that fits just above the washer and dryer. Screw ordinary shelf brackets to the wall and mount a board that just clears the tops.

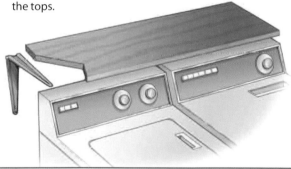

Great goof

Space is at a premium in our house, so we make use of every square foot. Last year I decided to build a shelf in the laundry room to store all the detergents, prewash additives and bleach bottles. I carefully measured the space between the washer and ceiling and calculated the number of shelves to fit the space. I got right to work. After finishing my shelving project, I stepped back to admire my space-saving genius just as my wife entered the room and lifted the washer lid. It hit the lower shelf and would only open halfway!

Laundry organizer

Make laundry day easier with this shelf for all your detergents, stain removers and other supplies. Build this simple organizer from 1x10 and 1x3 boards. If you have a basement laundry room, you may need to cut an access through the shelves for your dryer exhaust.

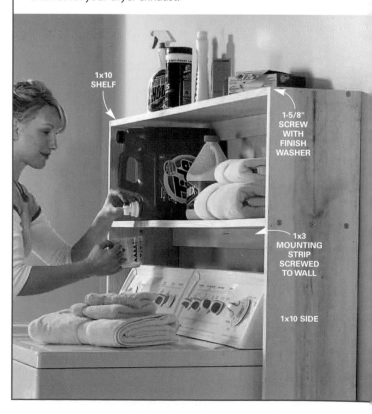

1x10 SHELF
1-5/8" SCREW WITH FINISH WASHER
1x3 MOUNTING STRIP SCREWED TO WALL
1x10 SIDE

Laundry room ironing center

To keep your ironing gear handy but out from underfoot, make this simple ironing center (about $25). All you need is a 10-ft. 1x8, a 2-ft. piece of 1x6 for the shelves and a pair of hooks to hang your ironing board.

Cut the back, sides, shelves and top. Align the sides and measure from the bottom 2 in., 14-3/4 in. and 27-1/2 in. to mark the bottom of the shelves (Photo 1). Before assembling the unit, use a jigsaw to cut a 1 x 1-in. dog ear at the bottom of the sides for a decorative touch.

Working on one side at a time, glue and nail the side to the back. Apply glue and drive three nails into each shelf, attach the other side and nail those shelves into place to secure them. Clamps are helpful to hold the unit together while you're driving nails. Center the top piece, leaving a 2-in. overhang on both sides, and glue and nail it into place (Photo 2). Paint or stain the unit and then drill pilot holes into the top face of each side of the unit and screw in the hooks to hold your ironing board. Mount the shelf on drywall using screw-in wall anchors.

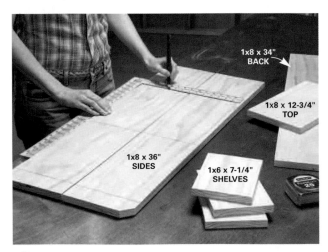

1 Place the sides next to each other and mark the shelf positions. For easier finishing, sand all the parts before marking and assembly.

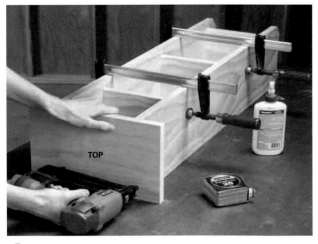

2 Glue and nail the back and shelves between the sides, then add the top. After painting or staining, screw on hooks for the ironing board.

Closet system

Annoyed by an overstuffed closet packed so tightly that you can't find your favorite shirt or shoes? Where the closet rod bends under the weight of all of "his" and "her" clothing?

If so, the simple closet organizing system shown here is a great solution. It utilizes the closet space much more efficiently by dividing your closet into zones that give your slacks, dresses, shirts, shoes and other items their own home. As a result, your clothing is better organized and you can find your party shirt or power skirt quickly and easily. It also prevents

"closet creep," where "her" clothing tends to infringe on "his" zone. (Or vice versa!) Overall, you'll get double the useful space of a traditional single pole and shelf closet.

Here you'll learn how to build this simple organizer, step-by-step, and how to customize it to fit closets of different sizes. It's designed for simplicity; you can build it in one weekend, even if you're a novice. However, to do a nice job, you should have experience using two basic power tools: a circular saw and a drill. A power miter box and an air-powered brad nailer make the job go a bit faster, but they aren't necessary.

Figure A
Closet organizer

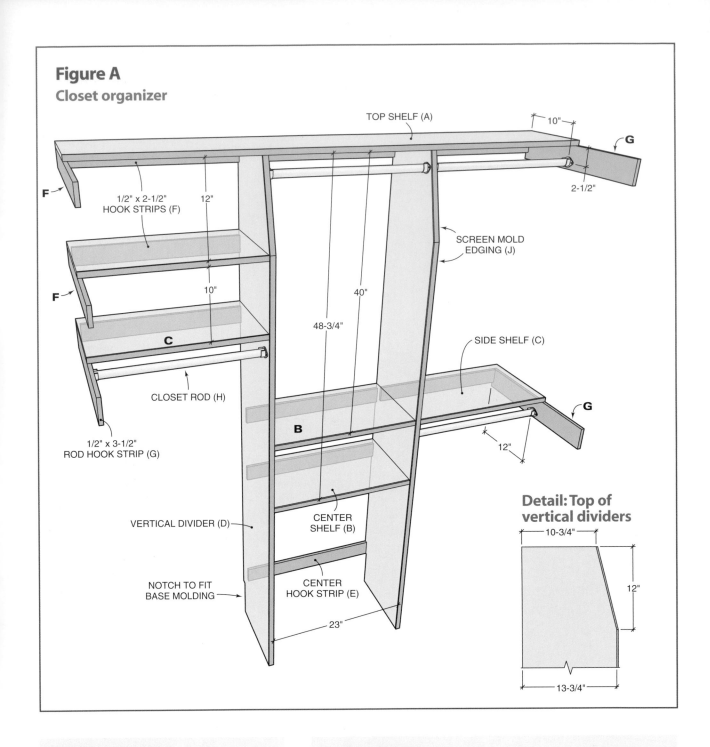

TOP SHELF (A)

10"

G

2-1/2"

1/2" x 2-1/2" HOOK STRIPS (F)

F

12"

10"

F

SCREEN MOLD EDGING (J)

40"

48-3/4"

C

SIDE SHELF (C)

CLOSET ROD (H)

1/2" x 3-1/2" ROD HOOK STRIP (G)

G

12"

B

VERTICAL DIVIDER (D)

CENTER SHELF (B)

NOTCH TO FIT BASE MOLDING

CENTER HOOK STRIP (E)

23"

Detail: Top of vertical dividers

10-3/4"

12"

13-3/4"

Materials list

Item	Qty.
3/4" x 4' x 8' sheets of oak plywood	1-1/2
1/2" x 2-1/2" hook strip	24'
1/2" x 3-1/2" hook strip	9'
1/4" x 3/4" x 8' screen molding	4
1-1/16" closet rod	8'
Pairs of rod holders	4
6d finishing nails	1 lb.

Cutting list

Key	Qty.	Size & Description
A	1	3/4" x 10-3/4" x closet length, plywood (top shelf)
B	2	3/4" x 13-1/2" x 23" plywood (center shelves)
C	3	3/4" x 13-1/2" x measured length plywood (side shelves)
D	2	3/4" x 13-3/4" x 82" plywood (vertical dividers)
E	4	1/2" x 2-1/2" x 23" (center hook strips)
F	7	1/2" x 2-1/2" x measured lengths (hook strips)
G	3	1/2" x 3-1/2" x closet depth (hook strips for rods)
H	4	1-1/16" x measured lengths (closet rods)
J		1/4" x 3/4" x measured lengths (screen molding)

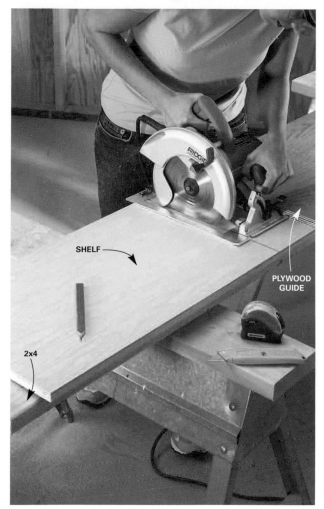

SHELF

PLYWOOD GUIDE

2x4

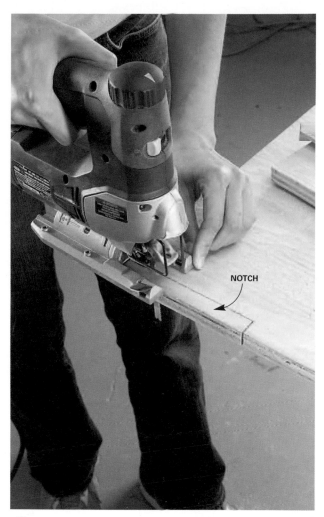

NOTCH

1 Measure your closet dimensions and cut the plywood vertical dividers and shelves to size (Figure A). Use a guide to make crosscuts perfectly square.

2 Measure the baseboard height and thickness and cut notches with a jigsaw on the vertical dividers to fit over it.

Don't buy it—build it!

While you may be tempted to buy a prefabricated organizer, it'll be surprisingly expensive when you tally up the cost of all the pieces. The materials for this organizer cost only $150. It uses 1-1/2 sheets of oak veneer plywood, plus several types of standard oak trim that you'll find at most home centers and lumberyards. (See the materials list on p. 112.) Keep in mind that if you use other wood species, you may have trouble finding matching trim, and you'll have to custom-cut it from solid boards on a table saw. If you choose to paint your organizer, you can use less expensive plywood and trim, and cut your expenses by about one-third.

Begin by measuring the width of your closet. The system shown here works best in a 6-ft. closet. If your closet only measures 5 ft., consider using a single vertical divider, rather than the two shown in Figure A.

Assemble the center unit

After referring to the cutting list (p. 112) and your closet dimensions, cut the plywood into two 13-3/4-in. pieces for the vertical dividers. If you plan to cut plywood with a circular saw, be sure to use a straightedge to get perfectly straight cuts.

Shown here are hook strips, used to attach the center unit and shelves to the closet walls, as well as for spacing the uprights (Figure A). If you want to save a bit of cash, you can cut these strips from the left-over plywood (and enjoy the gratification that comes from using the entire sheet). Cut the

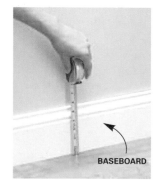

BASEBOARD

plywood to length using a factory plywood edge as a guide (Photo 1). Fully support your project with 2x4s so the cutoff doesn't fall and splinter. Also, for smoother cuts, use a sharp blade with at least 40 teeth.

You don't have to cut out the baseboard in the closet or even trim the back side of the dividers to fit its exact profile. The back of the organizer will be mostly out of sight, so square notches will do (Photo 2).

You'll have to trim the tops of the dividers back to 10-3/4 in. to make it easier to slide stuff onto the top shelf (unless you have an extra-deep closet). You can angle this cut to the first shelf point (Figure A, detail, p. 112).

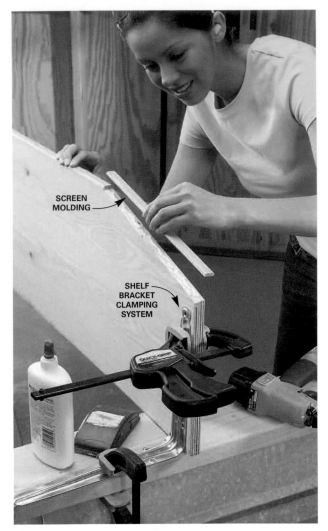

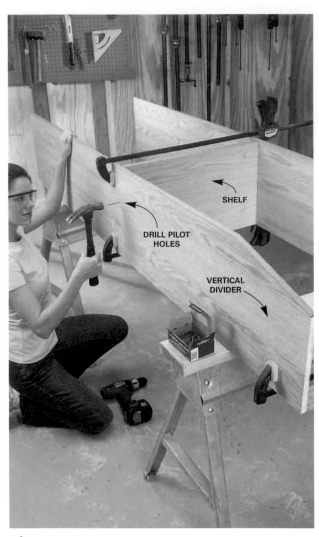

3 Smooth the cut plywood edges with 80-grit sandpaper and a block, then glue and tack 3/4-in. screen molding onto the edges that will show. Apply a stain or finish and let it dry.

4 Lay out the intermediate shelf positions with a square, spread glue on the shelf edges and nail the shelf to the dividers with 6d finish nails. Nail the 1/2-in. hook strips to the dividers as well.

tip When you're gluing and nailing your screen molding (Photo 3), have a damp cloth handy to promptly wipe away any glue ooze.

Apply the screen molding to hide the raw plywood edges on the dividers and shelves. You'll have to cut a 7-degree angle on the molding with a circular saw, jigsaw or miter saw to get a perfect fit on the dividers. Cut this angle first and when you get a nice fit, cut the other ends to length. You could also apply edge veneer (iron-on) or any other 3/4-in. wood strips to cover the edges.

Now sand all the parts to prepare them for finishing. A random orbital sander (starting at about $50) with 120-grit sandpaper will make quick work of this, but a few squares of sandpaper and a wood block will also do the trick. After sanding, wipe the surface of the wood with a clean cloth to remove dust.

It's easiest to apply your finish before assembly. Shown here is a warm fruitwood-tone Danish Finishing Oil. This type of finish brings out the natural grain of the wood, looks velvety

smooth, and is easy to renew when you scratch or scuff it. Use a small cloth to rub a generous amount of oil into the surface until the plywood and hook strips have an even sheen, and allow it to dry overnight.

tip To make perfect crosscuts on plywood, score your pencil line with a utility knife. This will give you a finer cut with less splintering of the veneer.

After the finish oil dries, assemble the center unit. Lightly mark the vertical dividers where the interior shelves and hook strips will be positioned and drill 1/8-in. pilot holes to simplify the nailing. Then spread a thin bead of wood glue onto the shelf ends and clamp the unit together. Use four 6d finish nails to pin the shelves securely (Photo 4), then countersink the nail heads with a nail set. Nails and glue are strong enough for holding garments and other light items, but if you plan to store items weighing more than about 50 lbs. on a closet shelf, put a cleat under the shelf to bear the weight.

Position one of the center unit's interior hook strips at the very top of the dividers and one above the bottom notches,

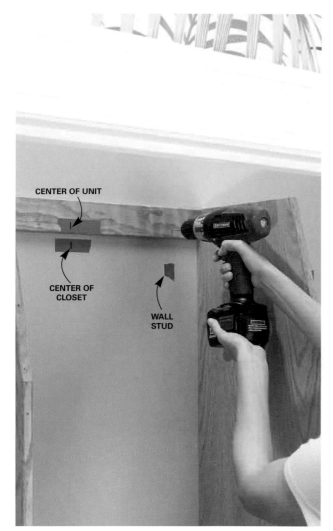

CENTER OF UNIT

CENTER OF
CLOSET

WALL
STUD

HOOK STRIPS

5 Set the center unit in the closet, level it with shims, predrill and tack the hook strips to the wall studs with 6d finish nails.

6 Level the hook strips with the top of the dividers, then predrill and nail them to the studs. Continue the strip around the closet sides.

and one under each shelf. The strips will shore up the unit and keep the plywood from bowing when you install it.

In the closet

If you have a thin carpet and pad, you can place the center unit directly on top of it. However, if you have a plush rug with a soft padding, stability is a concern. After determining the exact placement of your unit (by centering the unit on the midpoint of the closet; Photo 5), mark and cut out two 3/4-in.-wide slots in the carpet and pad so the dividers rest on the solid floor below.

Find the studs using a stud finder and mark them with masking tape. Also measure and mark the center of the wall on tape. This way you'll avoid marking up your walls. Set the unit in its position against the wall (Photo 5). Level and shim as necessary.

Predrill the hook strips with a 1/8-in. bit, then nail the unit to the studs. Level and nail on the remaining hook strips (Photo 6), starting with wider hook strips along the side walls to accommodate the hanging rod hardware (Figure A and Photo 8).

The inside walls of the closet will never be perfectly square because of joint compound and taping of the drywall corners. Measure your closet width and cut your shelf to the widest

dimension, then tilt the shelf into position. At the corners, mark a trim line along each end to achieve a snug fit (Photo 7).

Getting the top shelf over the central unit and onto the hook strips may take some finagling. Once you have the shelf resting squarely, drill pilot holes and nail it into the tops of the dividers and the hook strips (Photo 7).

Clothes rods and hardware

To avoid having to squeeze around shelves, install all your closet rod hardware before you put in the side shelves.

The hardware for the closet rods should be positioned about 1-1/2 to 2 in. down from the shelf above and about 10 to 12 in. from the back wall. These top rods were hung 10 in. from the back, which is good for pants, and the bottom rods, for shirts and blouses were hung at 12 in. If you want your top rod 12 in. out, make the top shelf 12 in. wide and trim less off the top of the vertical dividers.

Installing side shelves

To best secure the side shelves, sand the cut edge that will be in contact with the center unit with 100-grit paper. This will

TOP SHELF

ATTACH
ROD HOLDER

7 Trim the top shelf ends to fit the side walls, drop the shelf into place, and nail it to the tops of the vertical dividers and to the hook strip with 6d nails.

8 Sand the cut edge of the side shelves to prepare them for glue. Determine the exact shelf placement and drill pilot holes. Spread glue on the shelf end and secure it with 6d nails.

ROD HOLDER

WIDE
HOOK STRIP

break up any finishing oil and provide a cleaner surface for the glue.

Lay out the remaining shelves on their side wall hook strips and use a level to determine their exact position on the center unit.

Mark and drill the pilot holes through the center unit, then lift out the shelf and apply a thin bead of glue. To prevent smearing, put the center unit side in first while tipping up the wall side of the shelf. Keep a cloth handy to wipe up the inevitable glue smudges.

Nail the shelves in place and you're done.

Buyer's Guide

The shoe cabinets shown on the doors are available for $15 at IKEA stores. If you need help locating the nearest IKEA store, visit ikea.com.

The drawers and clothes hampers shown are available at Storables locations. Look for similar items at other organization stores and discount stores.

 tip Reduce bowing by storing plywood sheets flat rather than leaning them up on an edge.

Protect prime space

Your bedroom closet is valuable real estate, and the only way to protect it is to store off-season or rare-occasion clothing elsewhere.

Many people use garment bags, plastic bins (stored off the floor in a humidity-controlled basement) or a free-standing wardrobe. However, many mid-century homes have closets on the main level that are 4-1/2 ft. deep or better, and they're perfect candidates for off-season use.

Deep closets can fit double rods mounted parallel to each other in the front and the back. It's an ideal setup for tightly stashing off-season outfits. Add a rolling bin on the closet floor to store accessories, beachwear or ski gloves in Ziploc Big Bags (about $2 each). This will keep your bedroom closet clear and your active gear at hand.

Every clothing item should be handled annually and those not worn in a given season can be donated. Passing along unused attire creates the luxury of space and ease in any closet.

Clever clothing storage solutions

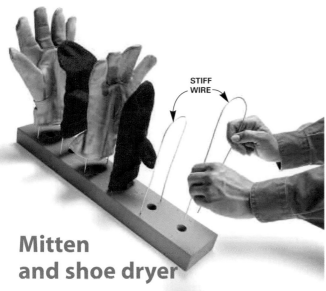

Mitten and shoe dryer

Drill pairs of 1/8-in. holes in a scrap of 2x4 and insert U-shaped pieces of galvanized 14-gauge wire (50 ft. sells for about $3 at home centers). If you have forced-air heat, drill 1-in. holes between the pairs of 1/8-in. holes using a spade bit, and set the rack on a register for fast drying.

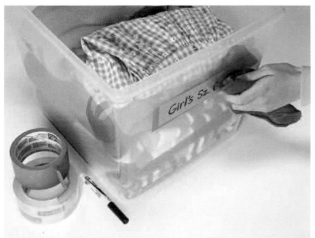

Erasable tape

When you need to continually update labels on items, such as storage boxes, create an erasable label. Put a piece of clear tape over masking tape and write on it using a dry-erase marker. The ink will wipe off easily, so you'll have to be careful not to smear it.

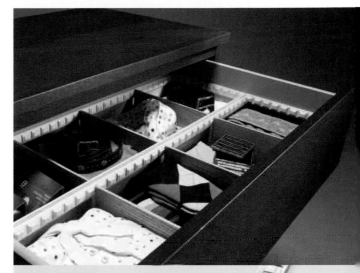

Drawer dividers

Here's a fast, inexpensive way to organize a messy drawer.

Cut standard dentil molding the width and length of your drawer, aligning the dentil slots on opposite sides. Glue or brad-nail the strips into place—one strip for dividers up to 2 in., two strips for larger dividers. For dividers, use oak or pine mull strip (sometimes called lattice) or rip 1/4-in. plywood.

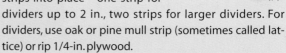

Dentil molding and 1/4-in.-thick mull strip are available at most home centers and lumberyards for roughly $1 per foot each (the system shown here cost $30). Sand the mull strip smooth with fine sandpaper, then wipe off all the dust. The wood can be left unfinished, or finished before it's installed in the drawer.

Glue dentil molding around the inside of the drawer and slip in dividers. Use additional molding to divide the space further.

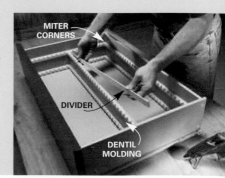

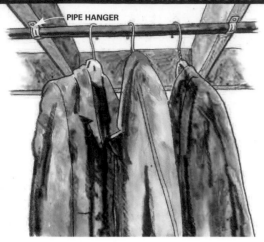

PIPE HANGER

Basement laundry rod

For more clothes-hanging space in your basement laundry area, make this rod from 3/4-in. copper or steel pipe and pipe hangers.

Turn a shelf into a clothes hanger rack

Sometimes you just need another place to hang clothes, like on the shelf over your washer and dryer. Turn the edge of that shelf into a hanger rack by predrilling some 3/4-in. plastic pipe and screwing it to the top of the shelf along the edge.

3/4" PLASTIC PIPE

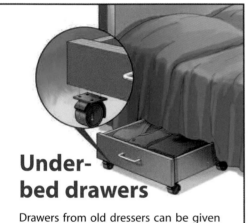

Under-bed drawers

Drawers from old dressers can be given new life as under-bed storage bins. Fasten small casters to the bottoms and slide the drawers under the bed to store seasonal clothes, extra blankets and more.

Great goof

One day I decided to put up new wire closet shelving. This was the first project in our new home and I was excited to get at it. I screwed the brackets to the wall without incident. We immediately stocked the shelves with our clothes, leaving the closet pocket door open so we could admire our work. The next day we could not close the pocket door! We tugged and tugged until it came off the track. You guessed it—our shelving screws ran through the finished drywall and were firmly embedded in the pocket door.

Now we have an even longer project list!

3/4" J-HOOK

7/8" DOWEL ROD

Quick-install clothes rod

If you need a clothes rod in the laundry room and you have exposed joists, check out this simple, solid and fast way to get it. Attach some 3/4-in. J-hooks (these are used for hanging pipe) to the joists and snap a 7/8-in. dowel rod in the curve.

5 Organize your outdoor stuff

Gardening and landscaping are rewarding endeavors that come with a tremendous amount of paraphernalia. Good tools and supplies are a must for lawn and garden projects, but if those items are scattered hither and yon, you may give up before you start!

Check out our best gardening tool holders and racks, plus complete instructions for a fun and functional outdoor storage locker.

Garden storage closet

If you don't have room in your yard for a large, freestanding shed, you can still create plenty of space for garden tools with a shed attached to the back or side of the house. If you're an experienced builder, you can build this shed in a couple of weekends. The one shown cost about $400, but you could save about $75 by using treated lumber, pine, and asphalt shingles instead of cedar.

Frame the walls and roof

Nail together the side walls, then square them with the plywood side panels. Overhang the panels 3/8 in. at the front—this will hide the gap at the corner when you hang the doors.

Join the two sides with the top and bottom plates and rim joists. The sides, top and bottom are all mirror images of each other except for the top front rim joist, which is set down 1/2 in. from the top so it stops the doors (Photo 1). Use screws to fasten the framework together except in the front where fasteners will be visible—use 2-1/2-in. casing nails there.

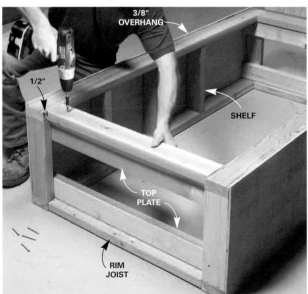

1 Frame and sheathe the walls, then join them with plates and joists. Use the best pieces of lumber in the front where they'll show.

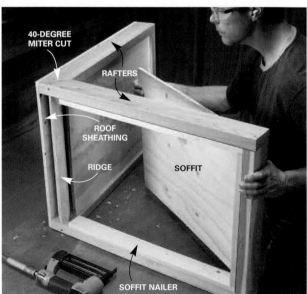

2 Build the roof on your workbench. Start with an L-shaped 2x4 frame, then add the nailers, soffit, sheathing and trim. Shingle with cedar or asphalt shingles.

Figure A

Garden closet construction details

The shed is made from three components—the roof, the walls and the doors, with edges covered by trim boards.

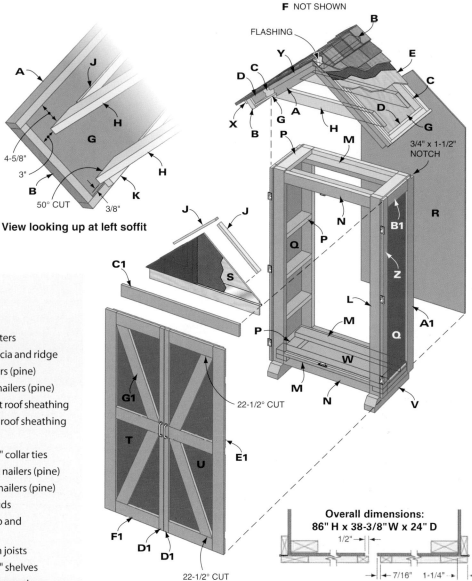

View looking up at left soffit

4-5/8"
3"
50° CUT
3/8"

22-1/2° CUT

22-1/2° CUT

3/4" x 1-1/2" NOTCH

Overall dimensions:
86" H x 38-3/8" W x 24" D

1/2"
7/16" 1-1/4"

LEFT DOOR   RIGHT DOOR

Door Detail—Top View

Cutting list

KEY	QTY.	SIZE & DESCRIPTION
A	4	1-1/2" x 3-1/2" x 32" rafters
B	3	1-1/2" x 3-1/2" x 20" fascia and ridge
C	4	3/4" x 2-1/2" x 27" nailers (pine)
D	2	3/4" x 2-1/2" x 18-1/2" nailers (pine)
E	1	1/2" x 23" x 31-7/8" right roof sheathing
F	1	1/2" x 23" x 32-1/4" left roof sheathing
G	2	1/2" x 20" x 28" soffit
H	2	1-1/2" x 3-1/2" x 38-3/8" collar ties
J	2	3/4" x 1-1/2" x 18" front nailers (pine)
K	2	3/4" x 1-1/2" x 23" rear nailers (pine)
L	4	1-1/2" x 3-1/2" x 64" studs
M	4	1-1/2" x 3-1/2" x 36" top and bottom plates
N	4	1-1/2" x 3-1/2" x 29" rim joists
P	10	1-1/2" x 3-1/2" x 13-1/2" shelves
Q	2	3/8" x 16-7/8" x 64" side panels
R	1	3/8" x 36-5/8" x 79-1/4" back panel
S	1	3/8" x 36" x 19-1/2" front panel
T	1	17-5/16" x 60-1/8" left door
U	1	18-5/16" x 60-1/8" right door
V	2	3-1/2" x 3-1/2" x 19-1/2" footings
W	1	13-3/8" x 35-7/8" plywood base
X	2	3/4" x 1-1/2" x 23" roof trim
Y	2	3/4" x 1-1/2" x 33-1/8" roof trim
Z	2	3/4" x 2-1/2" x 64" side battens
A1	2	3/4" x 3-1/2" x 64" rear side battens
B1	4	3/4" x 3-1/2" x 11-1/8" horizontal side battens
C1	1	3/4" x 3-1/2" x 38-3/8" front trim
D1	2	3/4" x 1-1/2" x 60-1/8" door edge
E1	2	3/4" x 3-1/2" x 60-1/8" door edge
F1	6	3/4" x 3-1/2" x 14-1/8" horizontal door trim
G1	4	3/4" x 3-1/2" x 28-3/8" (long edge to long edge) diagonal door trim

Materials list

Item	Qty.
3/8" x 4' x 8' rough-sawn exterior plywood	3
1/2" x 4' x 8' BC grade plywood	1
1x2 x 8' pine	1
1x2 x 8' cedar	3
1x3 x 8' pine	2
1x3 x 8' cedar	2
1x4 x 8' cedar	7
Cedar shakes	1 bundle
2x4 x 8' cedar	11
4x4 x 4' pressure treated	1

Item	Qty.
2-1/2" exterior screws	2 lbs.
1-5/8" exterior screws	1 lb.
2-1/2" galv. finish nails	1 lb.
1-1/2" galv. finish nails	1 lb.
1" narrow crown staples (for cedar shingles)	1 lb.
30-lb. felt	1 roll
10" x 10' roll aluminum flashing	1 roll
2-1/2" x 2-1/2" rust-resistant hinges	3 prs.
Magnetic catches	1 pr.
Handles	1 pr.

Note: Shown are rough-sawn cedar boards—which usually (but not always) measure 7/8 in. thick—for the trim. If you substitute pine, which measures 3/4 in., subtract 1/8 in. from each door width.

3 Set the completed roof on the shed base. Screw on the front and back panels to join the roof and the base.

ROOFING FELT

1" MINIMUM OVERLAP

FLASHING

4 Cover the front panel with roofing felt and shingles. Place metal flashing over the trim so water won't seep behind it.

Screw the 4x4 footings to the bottom plates, then nail on the plywood base. Cut and screw together the two pairs of rafters, then nail on the fascia and ridge boards. Nail on the roof sheathing and the soffit, butting the corners together (Photo 2). Screw on the collar ties at the points shown in Figure A, then screw on the front and rear nailers. Nail on the roof trim, staple on a layer of roofing felt, then shingle the roof. If you use cedar shingles, fasten them with narrow crown staples or siding nails. Leave 1/8-in. to 1/4-in. gaps between cedar shingles for expansion, and nail a strip of aluminum flashing across the ridge under the cap shingles.

Tip the shed upright, then set the roof on, aligning the front collar tie with the front rim joist and centering it side to side (Photo 3). Nail the cedar trim to the sides, aligning the 1x3s on the sides with the overhanging edge of plywood along the front edge. Glue and screw on the back and front siding panels to join the roof and base together. Use the back panel to square the structure and make it rigid.

Nail on the front trim piece, aligning it with the horizontal side battens (Z). Attach flashing and felt to the front panel, then cover it with cedar shakes (Photo 4).

Hang the doors

Finally, construct the doors (see Figure A detail, p. 121), cut the hinge mortises (see below) and hang the doors. Leave a 1/8-in. gap between the doors and trim along the top. Paint or stain if desired, then set the shed against the house on several inches of gravel. Add or take away gravel under the footings until the shed is tight against the siding and the gap above the doors is even. Screw the shed to the studs in the wall to keep it from tipping. Drill two 1/2-in. holes for the screws through the plywood near the rim joists, then loosely fasten the shed to the wall with 2-1/2-in. screws and large fender washers so the shed can move up and down when the ground freezes and thaws.

How to mortise a hinge

Mark the hinge locations on the doorjamb, then on the door, less 1/8 in. for clearance at the top of the door. Separate the hinge leaves, then align the edge of the leaf with the edge of the door or jamb. Predrill and fasten the leaf, then cut along all three edges with a razor knife to about the same depth as the hinge leaf (Photo 1).

Remove the hinge and make a series of angled cuts to establish the depth of the mortise (Photo 2). Turn the chisel over and clean out the chips using light hammer taps.

Holding the chisel with the beveled front edge against the wood, chip out the 1/4-in. sections. Check the fit of the hinge leaf and chisel out additional wood until the leaf sits flush.

If the hinges don't fit back together perfectly when you hang the door, tap the leaves up or down (gently) with a hammer.

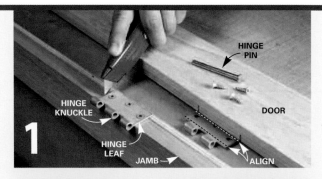

HINGE PIN

HINGE KNUCKLE

HINGE LEAF

JAMB

DOOR

ALIGN

1

2

DEPTH OF HINGE LEAF

Clever outdoor storage solutions

Overhead storage for garden tools

Rakes, shovels, brooms and other long-handled tools seem to be in the way no matter how they're stored in the garage. Here's a rack that works: Cut two pieces of plywood about 12 in. x 48 in. and drill matching 2-in. holes in each, spaced about 6 in. apart. Mount the racks on crossties below your garage roof rafters.

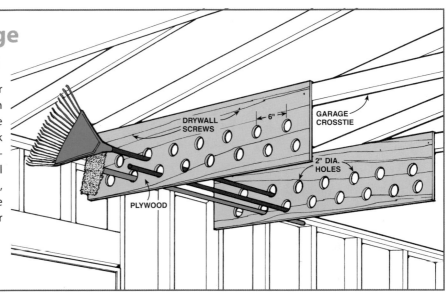

DRYWALL SCREWS

6"

GARAGE CROSSTIE

2" DIA. HOLES

PLYWOOD

Garage organizer

Cut an old hose into 7-in. pieces, slit them, and nail them to the wall to make good holders for handled tools in the garage.

Two-minute tool rack

One way to get rid of clutter in your storage shed or garage is to screw 16-in. scrap 2x4s at a slight upward angle to each side of a wall stud. They will hold a wide variety of yard tools.

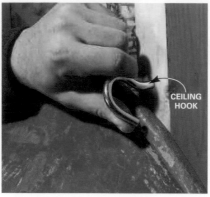

Wheelbarrow rack

Hang your wheelbarrow on the garage wall to free up floor space. Center a 2-ft. 1x4 across two studs, 2 ft. above the floor. Tack it into place, then drive 3-in. screws through metal mending plates and the 1x4, into the studs. Leave about 3/4 in. of the plate sticking above the 1x4 to catch the rim. Rest the wheelbarrow on the 1x4 as shown, and mark the studs 1 in. above the wheelbarrow bucket. Drill pilot holes and screw ceiling hooks into the studs. Twist the hooks so they catch on the wheelbarrow lip and hold it in place.

Lawn tool carrier

An old golf bag with a cart makes a perfect holder for your garden tools. The large wheels make it easy to haul the tools over long distances and rough terrain.

Yard tool organizer

Create a simple long-handled tool hanger out of two 1x4s. On the first one, drill a series of 2-in. holes along the edge of the board. The trick is to center each hole about 1 in. from the edge. That leaves a 1-1/2-in. slot in the front that you can slip the handles through. Space the holes to accommodate whatever it is you're hanging. Screw that board to another 1x4 for the back and add 45-degree brackets to keep it from sagging. If you wish, pound nails into the vertical board to hang even more stuff. No more tripping over the shovels to get to the rakes!

Propane tank carrier

When you take your 20-lb. propane tank to be filled, does it always roll around in the trunk of your car? To solve the problem, stick it in an old milk crate. The crate's wide, flat base keeps the tank stable.

Garden tool hideaway

A mailbox near your garden provides a convenient home for tools. A small mailbox like this one costs less than $10 at hardware stores and home centers. King-size models cost about $25.

Bulb storage solution

Tender bulbs that must be overwintered indoors are hard to keep organized. These include canna lilies, freesias, caladiums, gladioluses, dahlias and tuberous begonias. Keep track of who's who by storing them in egg cartons, with each bulb identified on the top of the carton. The cartons even have ventilation holes that help prevent rot and mildew.

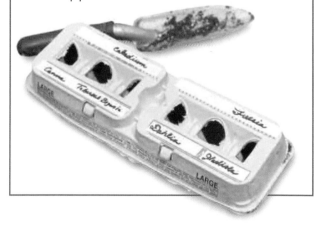

Hose caddy

Here's an easy way to store unwieldy garden hoses without strangling yourself. Coil them up in a round laundry basket or plastic bucket. Then hang the basket or bucket on the garage wall or slide it into an obscure corner.

Milk jug tarp weights

Use milk jugs partially filled with water or sand to weight the edges of a tarp. It looks weird, but for awkwardly shaped stuff it works better than trying to tie the tarp down.

No-tip garbage cans

There really is a simple way to keep those garbage cans from getting blown or knocked over. For each garbage can, all you need are two 3/4-in. screw eyes and a 30-in. hook-end elastic cord from the hardware store.

Lid leash

Tired of losing your garbage can lid because the wind blew it away or because it skittered away when you tried to knock it off when your hands were full of trash? Drill a small hole just below the rim of the can, and another near the center of the lid. Then thread a 24-in. length of rope through the holes, and knot the ends as shown. The lid will always be right there when you go to put it back.

Storing your lawn mower for the winter

Gasoline left in your mower during storage can deteriorate and leave gum deposits that clog the fuel system. There are two storage methods: completely draining the system or leaving it completely filled with fresh, stabilized gasoline.

Most manufacturers of newer mowers recommend draining the gas completely. Do this by opening the drain valve or drain bolt on the carburetor bowl and draining the gas into a container. If your carburetor doesn't have a drain valve, check with the manufacturer or lawn mower repair center for instructions.

Older lawn mowers with a foam filter and carburetor that's screwed to the top of the gas tank should be filled with stabilized fuel for the winter. Purchase a container of fuel stabilizer, available at hardware stores, home centers, gas stations or lawn mower service centers, and mix as recommended with fresh gas. Fill the empty lawn mower tank with the stabilized gas and run the mower for about 10 minutes. Then top off the fuel tank with stabilized gas and shut the fuel valve. Check your owner's manual for storage instructions.

Backyard storage locker

Lawn and garden tools present a paradox: You can never find the right tool when you need it, then when you aren't looking for it, it's in your way. This simple-to-build locker solves both problems. It stores tools so they're easy to find, and it does so in a convenient location in your yard so they're not cluttering your garage.

The locker's 4 x 8-ft. footprint provides ample room to store space-hogging items like walk-behind lawn mowers and snowblowers. Long- and short-handled garden tools, lawn treatments and potting materials also fit nicely inside.

Here you'll learn how to build this attractive storage locker using easy construction techniques. It's a great project for beginners looking to expand their building skills.

Time, tools and money

You can build and paint this locker in a weekend, although you might need another half day to give the pressure-treated trim a second coat of paint. The straightforward construction requires only basic power tools—a circular saw with a standard carbide blade and a drill. An air compressor and nail gun aren't necessary but will make the framing and trim work easier (and faster!).

For this locker, fiber cement panels were used for siding because they resist rot and hold paint well (the panels come

A clear roof lets in the sunshine

These clear plastic roof panels let in sunlight so you can easily see inside. They're lightweight, faster to install than asphalt shingles and don't need sheathing underneath. You can cut them with a carbide blade in a circular saw. And best of all, they won't peel or tear like shingles, and they last for decades. The downside is they're not in stock at most home centers. You may have to special order them.

PEA GRAVEL

SLEEPER

1 Lay sleepers over gravel to create a flat foundation fast. Add or remove gravel until the sleepers are level.

SLEEPER

2 Screw the floor framing to the sleepers at each corner. Then double-check the floor for level.

BRACE

3 Build the walls and screw them to the floor. Attach temporary bracing to hold the walls plumb.

primed). If you substitute plywood panels, be aware that they'll eventually rot along the bottoms where they're in ground contact. Corrugated plastic panels were used for the roof because they let in light and are easy to install. Materials for this locker cost about $500.

Preconstruction planning

A flat or nearly flat site (less than a 6-in. slope over 6 ft.) is ideal for this storage locker. You can add gravel or stack up several sleepers on one side if your site has a steeper slope, but the doors need 3 ft. of space to open. If the locker faces a steep slope, you'll have to dig away the ground in front of the doors so they can fully open.

You can find all the materials except perhaps the roof panels at most home centers. Shown are Sequentia panels from Crane Composites (cranecomposites.com/sequentia), which are available in several colors and clear.

Buy treated trim material a few weeks early and let it dry. Otherwise, the wet wood will shrink and won't hold paint. Make sure to use galvanized nails or exterior screws because they won't corrode.

Lay the floor on sleepers

Start by digging parallel trenches 10 in. wide by 6 in. deep and centered 3 ft. 6 in. apart. If the ground is slightly sloped, dig out any high areas between the trenches so you can (later) place a level across the sleepers.

Fill the trenches with pea gravel so they're roughly level. Then cut treated 2x6 sleepers to size and set them over the gravel so the outside edges are 4 ft. apart. Place a 4-ft. level over

Materials list

ITEM	QTY.	ITEM	QTY.
2x4 x 8' treated pine (floor joists)	6	1x4 x 10' treated pine (corner boards and door top, bottom and center trim)	8
1/2" x 4' x 8' treated plywood (floor)	1		
2x4 x 8' pine (studs, plates, supports, trimmers, rafters, purlins)	16	1x4 x 8' treated pine (door trim)	4
2x4 x 8' treated pine (plates)	2	2x4 x 12' treated pine (door casing)	1
2x6 x 8' pine (header, sleepers)	3	1-5/16" x 2-1/4" x 8' pine molding (astragal)	1
2x10 x 8' pine (shelves)	2	Fence brackets	10
5/16" x 4' x 8' fiber cement (siding)	6	1-1/2" hex head panel screws	1 box
		4d galvanized nails	1 lb.
5/8" x 1" x 8' plugs	3	6d galvanized nails	5 lbs.
5/8" x 5/8" x 100" supports (quarter round)	1	8d galvanized nails	5 lbs.
		3" exterior screws	1 lb.
27" x 9' roof panels	3	16d galvanized nails	5 lbs.
1x4 x 10' pine (fascia)	3	4" T-hinge	4
1x3 x 10' pine (fascia)	3	Gate pull	1
		Gate latch slide bolt	1
		Pea gravel (50-lb. bags)	10

Figure A
Storage locker

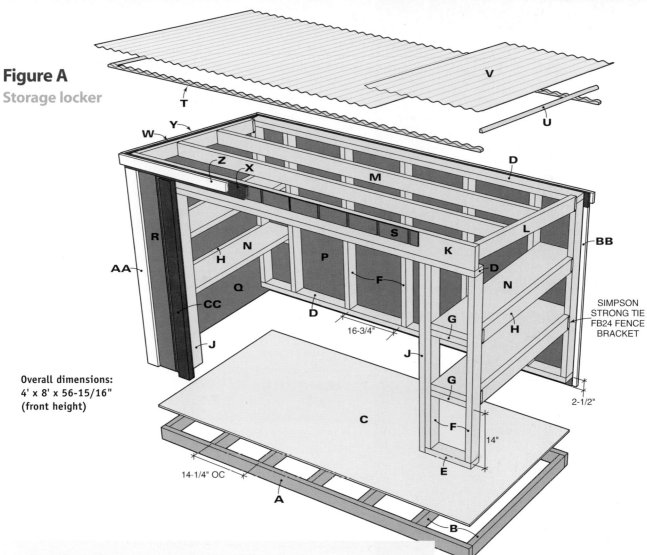

Overall dimensions:
4' x 8' x 56-15/16"
(front height)

SIMPSON
STRONG TIE
FB24 FENCE
BRACKET

2-1/2"

14"

16-3/4"

14-1/4" OC

Cutting list

KEY	PCS.	SIZE & DESCRIPTION
A	2	2x4 x 96" treated (rim joists)
B	7	2x4 x 45" treated (joists)
C	1	1/2" x 48" x 96" treated (floor)
D	3	2x4 x 96" (plates); one treated
E	2	2x4 x 12-1/4" treated (bottom plates)
F	11	2x4 x 45-3/4" (studs)
G	8	2x4 x 9-1/4" (shelf supports)
H	4	2x4 x 40-7/8" (purlins)
J	2	2x4 x 47-1/4" (trimmers)
K	1	2x6 x 96" (header)
L	2	2x4 x 44" (rafters)*
M	2	2x4 x 93" (mid-beams)
N	4	2x10 x 48" (shelves)
P	2	5/16" x 48" x 51-1/4" (siding)
Q	2	5/16" x 48" x 57" (siding)*
R	2	5/16" x 13-3/4" x 56-3/4" (siding)
S	2	5/16" x 34-1/4" x 3-5/16" (siding)

KEY	PCS.	SIZE & DESCRIPTION
T	2	5/8" x 1" x 99-5/8" (plugs)
U	2	5/8" x 5/8" x 50" (supports)*
V	5	27" x 54" (roof panels)
W	2	1x4 x 50" (fascia)*
X	2	1x4 x 98-1/8" (fascia)
Y	2	1x3 x 52" (fascia)*
Z	2	1x3 x 99-5/8" (fascia)
AA	4	1x4 x 53-7/16" treated (corner boards)
BB	4	1x4 x 48-1/8" (corner boards)*
CC	2	2x4 x 53-7/16" treated (casings)
DD	4	5/16" x 33-15/16" x 26-5/8" (panels)
EE	8	1x4 x 46-1/4" treated (trim)
FF	8	1x4 x 33-15/16" treated (trim)
GG	4	1x4 x 26-15/16" treated (trim)
HH	1	1-5/16" x 2-1/4" x 53-1/4" (astragal)

*Cut to fit

Figure B
Door detail

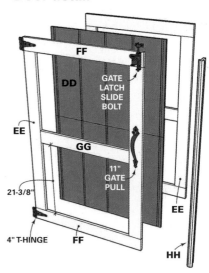

GATE LATCH SLIDE BOLT

11" GATE PULL

21-3/8"

4" T-HINGE

4 Install the purlins. Inexpensive fence brackets make fastening the purlins easy.

FENCE BRACKET
PURLIN
SHELF SUPPORT
FENCE BRACKET

5 Nail the rafters to the header and align them with the top of the back wall to create a flat plane for the roof.

RAFTER
BACK WALL

6 Nail on the siding. Support the heavy siding panels with temporary nails placed 1-1/2 in. from the bottom of the floor framing.

one of the sleepers. Level it, then adjust the second sleeper until it's level with the first (Photo 1).

Frame the floor on your driveway or other flat surface with treated lumber using 16d nails or 3-in. screws, following Figure A on p. 129. Lay a full sheet of 1/2-in. 4 x 8-ft. treated plywood over the floor frame. Adjust the floor frame so the corners are aligned with the edges of the plywood, then fasten the plywood using 8d nails or 1-1/2-in. screws. Snap chalk lines at the floor joist locations to make them easy to find. Drive fasteners every 6 to 8 in. along the edges and every 12 in. in the field.

Place the floor over the sleepers, align the corners, then drive 3-in. screws at an angle into the sleepers (Photo 2).

Frame the walls and roof

Build the front and back walls following Figure A. Use treated lumber for the bottom plates and the door trimmers. Attach the assembled walls to the floor with 16d nails or 3-in. screws. Drive the fasteners near the outside edge to ensure they go into the underlying framing, not just into the plywood.

Have a helper place a level on a stud near one end of a wall. When the wall is plumb, fasten temporary bracing between the wall and the floor (Photo 3).

If you're not an experienced builder, toenailing the purlins into place can be tricky since it's hard to drive nails and keep the purlins at their marks. Avoid this frustration by using fence brackets. Nail them to the outside studs on the front and back walls with 8d nails, keeping the tops 1-1/2 in. above the top of the shelf supports. This keeps the tops of the purlins and the shelves (installed next) aligned for a flat surface.

Cut the purlins to size, set them into the brackets and drive 4d nails through the bracket holes (Photo 4). Cut the shelves to size and fasten them with 8d nails. It's important to install the shelves now since they won't fit after the siding is on.

Set the header in place, flush with the outside of the front wall. Drive 16d nails or 3-in. screws through the underside of the top plate into the header every 6 to 8 in.

To mark the angled end of the rafters, hold them in place alongside the header and the back wall. Mark the rafters and cut them to size. Use the fence brackets to hold the rafters in place on the back wall. Nail the brackets so the top is slightly above the top of the wall.

Nail the rafters in the brackets. Hold the opposite end flush with the top and side of the header, then face-nail it with two 16d nails or 3-in. screws.

To frame the roof, install the rafters (Photo 5). Cut two mid-beams at 93 in. Mark the rafters at the one-third and two-third distances between the walls. Place the mid beams at the marks and attach them with 16d nails or 3-in. screws.

Side with fiber cement

Use a carbide saw blade in a circular saw for cutting the fiber cement siding panels—and be sure to wear a mask. Cutting cement siding is extremely dusty. And be prepared—the 4 x 8-ft. panels are heavy.

Keep the siding 1-1/2 in. from the bottom of the locker to avoid direct contact with the ground.

Cut panels for the back and front walls following Figure A. Install the front panels, starting at a corner. Then install the back panels so they butt together over the middle stud on the wall. Don't worry that the panels don't fully cover the corners. You'll cover them later with trim.

Nail the panels with 8d nails. Drive the nails snug with a smooth-face hammer so you won't mar the siding. Drive nails straight, not at an angle. Keep nails 3/8 in. from panel edges and 2 in. from corners. Hold the side panels in place (don't nail them yet) and mark them along the top of the rafters. Cut them to size and nail them into place (Photo 6).

Add the trim

Painting along the roof panels is a pain, so it's best to paint the trim now. If you're using two colors, paint everything—you won't have to cut in with paint later.

Install 1x4 fascia along the top of the locker. Start with the back, then add the sides, then the front. Hold each piece in place to mark the angle and cut it to size, then attach it with 8d nails before moving on to the next piece. Then cut and install 1x3 fascia over the 1x4 fascia.

Use treated lumber for the corner boards since they're in ground contact. Cut the corner boards to size and nail them into place with 8d nails. Nail the boards on the sides first, then install the boards on the back and front walls, overlapping the side boards (Photo 7).

Cut and nail treated 2x4 door supports flush with the door opening, butted against the fascia. Use 16d nails. The door supports stick out a little proud of the fascia, but the extra thickness is needed to support the doors.

Install a clear roof

Before installing the roof, place wooden panel plugs flush with the outside of the fascia along the front and the back walls. Drill pilot holes through the peaks and nail the plugs into place with 4d nails. The plugs conform to the shape of the roof panels, sealing the openings to keep out the birds and the bees. For roof support along the sides, install supports (quarter round).

Cut the 9-ft.-long roof panels in half with a circular saw. Run a generous bead of silicone caulk along both plugs for 27 in., then set the panels in place so there's an equal overhang on the front and back and about 2 in. on the side.

Drill 1/8-in. pilot holes through every third peak at the plugs and the mid-beams, then insert 1-1/2-in. hex-head panel screws.

Caulk along the edge of the installed roof panel and the panel plugs (Photo 8). Then install the next roof panel. Overlap the panels by 3 in. When you get to the end, cut the last panel to size.

Paint 'er up!

Build the doors using treated lumber and following Figure B. Use scrap siding panels for the door panels since the middle 1x4 hides the gap. Assemble the doors with 6d nails driven at a slight angle so they don't poke through the opposite side. Make sure the seams in the top and bottom scrap pieces are aligned before nailing them into place.

If you haven't painted the locker yet, now is a good time. Install the doors. Start by nailing a scrap piece of wood in front of the opening so the top is 1-1/2 in. from the bottom of the locker. Drill pilot holes and attach heavy-duty door hinges to the top and bottom of both doors. Set both doors in place over the scrap lumber. Insert shims so the doors don't pinch at the top and side, then attach the hinges to the door supports with screws (Photo 9). Add handles and a lock as desired.

7 Trim the storage locker, starting with the fascia. Then add the corner boards.

8 Lay a heavy bead of caulk over the plug strip before screwing on the roof panel.

9 Hold the doors in perfect position with shims. Then screw on the hinges.

Shelves & Bookcases
Hints, tips & goofs

Measure twice!

A few years ago, I needed a bookcase for all the books we were accumulating. I decided that I'd make it floor-to-ceiling so we wouldn't run out of room anytime soon. After I built the bookcase, I brought it into the room to tip it into place. No matter how I angled the bookcase, the ceiling was too low for it. The only way to salvage this nice woodworking project was to cut off the bottom. I did save the pieces and luckily was able to use them in our new home (with higher ceilings) three years later.

Between studs shelving

Store smaller containers—spray paint, putty cans, glue bottles—right in the wall! Screw shelf brackets (6-ft. lengths cost $1.50 each at home centers) to the studs, then install shelves, cut from standard 1x4 boards, on adjustable clips ($2 for a bag of 12). The boards fit perfectly; there's no need to saw them to width.

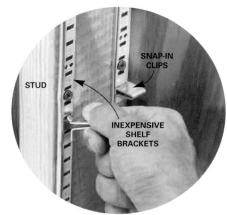

SNAP-IN CLIPS

STUD

INEXPENSIVE SHELF BRACKETS

Sturdier shelf trick

1/8"-DEEP SAW CUTS

Ordinary clip-in-place shelf brackets with slotted metal supports can hold a lot of weight. But sometimes they're unstable and can be easily knocked loose. The play in the slots allows the bracket and shelf to shift from side to side. To prevent this, use your circular saw to cut 1/8-in.-deep slots into the undersides of the shelves, aligned with each bracket. When the shelf is assembled, the brackets fit into the slots, eliminating the sway.

Display shelving

Assemble this simple shelf from 1x4s and tempered glass. Fasten the side boards to the 4-ft. back sections with wood glue and 6d finish nails. Paint the brackets and screw them to wall studs. Buy round-cornered tempered glass shelves and slide them into place.

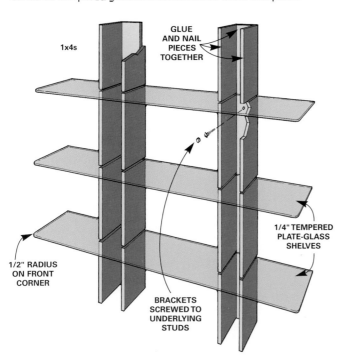

1x4s

GLUE AND NAIL PIECES TOGETHER

1/2" RADIUS ON FRONT CORNER

BRACKETS SCREWED TO UNDERLYING STUDS

1/4" TEMPERED PLATE-GLASS SHELVES

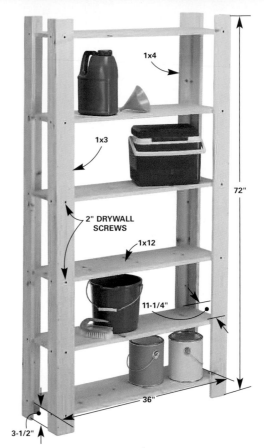

1x4

1x3

2" DRYWALL SCREWS

1x12

11-1/4"

72"

36"

3-1/2"

Utility shelves

This sturdy, freestanding shelf unit is made from any inexpensive standard width, 3/4-in.-thick lumber for the legs, and plywood or particleboard for the shelves. Glue and nail the four L-shaped legs together with 6d finish nails. Clamp the shelves in place, getting them evenly spaced and level, then secure each shelf with eight 2-in. screws through the legs.

Sliding bookend

To corral shelf-dwelling books or CDs that like to wander, cut 3/4-in.-thick hardwood pieces into 6-in. squares. Use a band saw or jigsaw to cut a slot along one edge (with the grain) that's a smidgen wider than the shelf thickness. Stop the notch 3/4 in. from the other edge. Finish the bookend and slide it on the shelf.

Shoddy shelving

I was using my brad nailer to assemble large bookshelves. As the final boards slipped tightly into place, I was feeling delighted with the precision of my cuts and stood back to admire my handiwork. Within seconds, all the shelves noisily gave way. Apparently perfect craftsmanship is worthless if you don't remember to put nails in your nail gun.

Petite shelves

Turn a single 3-ft.-long, 1x12 hardwood board into some small shelves to organize a desktop or counter. Cut off a 21-in.-long board for the shelves, rip it in the middle to make two shelves, and cut 45-degree bevels on the two long front edges with a router or table saw. Bevel the ends of the other board, then cut dadoes (grooves cut into the wood) with a router or a table saw with a dado blade (cut a dado on scrap and test-fit the shelves first!). Rip it into four narrower boards, two at 1-3/8 in. wide and two at 4 in. Finish, then assemble with brass screws and finish washers.

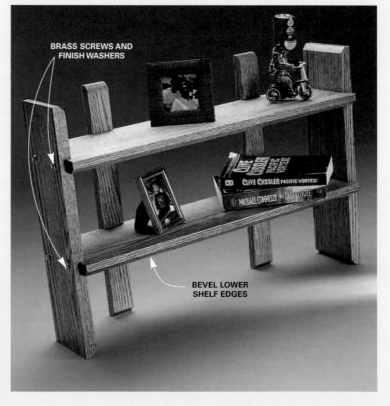

BRASS SCREWS AND FINISH WASHERS

BEVEL LOWER SHELF EDGES

CUT DADOES BEFORE RIPPING LEGS

10" 1x4

Heavy-duty shelf brackets

Build two super-strong shelf brackets with a steel-framing track. Use tin snips to cut two 41-in. lengths. Then cut V-notches 1 ft. in from both ends. Screw one end of the track to the wall studs with a 10-in. 1x4 and then fold the track at the notches, bringing the ends together. Reinforce all the corners with steel framing screws. Set a shelf board on top. **Caution: Steel stud track has sharp edges. Wear gloves to protect your hands.**

Build sturdy, simple shelves, custom sized to hold boxes or other storage containers.

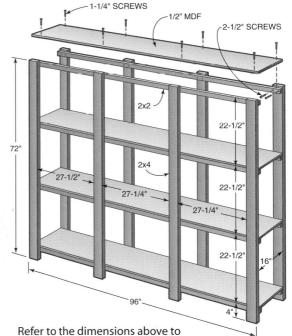

1-1/4" SCREWS · 1/2" MDF · 2-1/2" SCREWS · 2x2 · 2x4 · 72" · 27-1/2" · 27-1/4" · 27-1/4" · 22-1/2" · 22-1/2" · 22-1/2" · 16" · 96" · 4"

Sturdy storage shelves

Store-bought shelving units are either hard to assemble, flimsy or awfully expensive. Here's a better solution. These shelves are strong, easy to build and cost about $70. The sturdy shelf unit is sized to hold standard bankers' boxes ($4 each). If you want deeper storage, build the shelves 24 in. deep and buy 24-in.-deep boxes. If you prefer to use plastic storage bins, measure the size of the containers and modify the shelf and upright spacing to fit.

Refer to the dimensions above to mark the location of the horizontal 2x2 on the back of four 2x4s. Also mark the position of the 2x4 uprights on the 2x2s. Then simply line up the marks and screw the 2x2s to the 2x4s with pairs of 2-1/2-in. wood screws. Be sure to keep the 2x2s and 2x4s at right angles. Rip a 4 x 8-ft. sheet of 1/2-in. MDF, plywood or OSB into 16-in.-wide strips and screw it to the 2x2s to connect the two frames and form the shelving unit.

Good money down the drain

My father loves home improvement projects, so while he was visiting, I asked him if he would install shelving in our attached garage. He measured everything and went and picked up the supplies. We couldn't find the stud finder, so he decided to just tap on the wall and find the studs the old-fashioned way. I left to run errands and when I came back, the shelving was up. It looked great! He'd saved me a pile of money. Later, my kids noticed water stains on the wall behind the new shelving. After investigating, we noticed that when the toilet was flushed upstairs, the leak would appear again. I called a plumber and he discovered that a screw had gone through the PVC waste pipe behind the wall. My money savings was literally "down the drain" after I'd paid the plumber and drywaller to fix the goof.

Portable bookshelf

Here's a cool knock-down shelf for a dorm room or den. You just slide the shelves between the dowels, and they pinch the shelves to stiffen the bookshelf. It works great if you're careful about two things:

- Make the space between the dowel holes exactly 1/16 in. wider than the thickness of the shelf board.
- Be sure the shelf thickness is the same from end to end and side to side.

After test-fitting a dowel in a trial hole (you want a tight fit), drill holes in a jig board so the space between the holes is your shelf thickness plus 1/16 in. Clamp the jig board on the ends of the risers and drill the holes. Cut the dowels 1-3/4 in. longer than the shelf width, then dry assemble (no glue). Mark the angled ends of the risers parallel to the shelves and cut off the tips to make the risers sit flat. Disassemble and glue the dowels in the riser holes. When the glue dries, slide the shelves in and load them up.

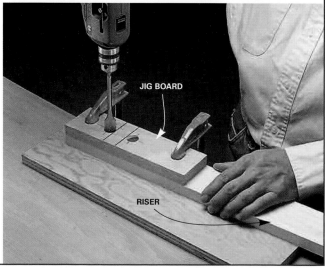

Cutting list

Perfectly flat 1x12 lumber or plywood
2 shelves: 11-1/4 in. wide x 3 ft. long
4 risers: 2-1/4 in. wide x 24 in. long
8 dowels: 3/4 in. dia. x 13 in. long

Elegant & easy bookcases

Build a pair in one weekend for $300

This is one of those rare woodworking projects that has it all: high style at a low cost, and fast, easy construction that delivers sturdy, lasting results. This bookcase design is versatile, too. You can easily make it shorter or taller, wider or deeper. With a little know-how, you can even adapt the building methods to other projects, like the fireplace mantel shown here.

You could save a few hours of work by building just one bookcase, but there's a financial incentive to build two. By mostly using the plywood left over from the first bookcase, you can get a second one for half price. The materials for one oak bookcase will cost you about $200; two will cost about $300. If you choose cherry or birch, expect to spend an extra $100 or more on materials.

You'll need a table saw and a miter saw for this project. A pneumatic brad nailer will make the job faster and easier. All the materials are at home centers. You may not find the solid wood panel shown here as the bookshelf top (made from glued-together boards). You could use oak stair tread material or glue boards together. Also the home center may not carry the board widths listed here, but you can easily rip wider boards to width.

Cut the plywood parts

To get started, rip the plywood parts to width on a table saw. If cutting full sheets is difficult in your small shop, cut the parts slightly oversized with a circular saw and then trim them on the table saw. Rip two 9-in.-wide planks of 3/4-in. plywood (for the shelves) and two from the 1/2-in. plywood (for the sides). Then cut them to length. To make the crosscuts with a miter saw, use a stop block (Photo 1, p. 139).

Next, drill the screw holes in the sides using a 3/32-in. bit (Photo 2). Measuring from the bottom, mark the screw holes at 3-3/8, 16-1/8, 26-7/8, 37-5/8, 48-3/8 and 58-1/8 in. Position the holes 1 in. from the edges so the screw heads will be covered by the stiles later.

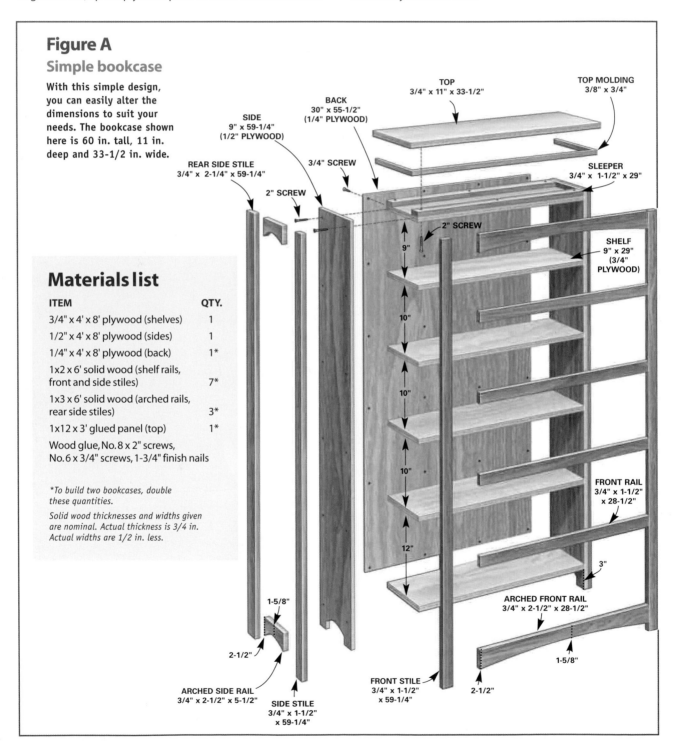

Figure A
Simple bookcase

With this simple design, you can easily alter the dimensions to suit your needs. The bookcase shown here is 60 in. tall, 11 in. deep and 33-1/2 in. wide.

TOP
3/4" x 11" x 33-1/2"

TOP MOLDING
3/8" x 3/4"

BACK
30" x 55-1/2"
(1/4" PLYWOOD)

SIDE
9" x 59-1/4"
(1/2" PLYWOOD)

REAR SIDE STILE
3/4" x 2-1/4" x 59-1/4"

3/4" SCREW

SLEEPER
3/4" x 1-1/2" x 29"

2" SCREW

2" SCREW

9"

SHELF
9" x 29"
(3/4" PLYWOOD)

10"

10"

10"

FRONT RAIL
3/4" x 1-1/2" x 28-1/2"

12"

3"

ARCHED FRONT RAIL
3/4" x 2-1/2" x 28-1/2"

1-5/8"

Materials list

ITEM	QTY.
3/4" x 4' x 8' plywood (shelves)	1
1/2" x 4' x 8' plywood (sides)	1
1/4" x 4' x 8' plywood (back)	1*
1x2 x 6' solid wood (shelf rails, front and side stiles)	7*
1x3 x 6' solid wood (arched rails, rear side stiles)	3*
1x12 x 3' glued panel (top)	1*

Wood glue, No. 8 x 2" screws, No. 6 x 3/4" screws, 1-3/4" finish nails

*To build two bookcases, double these quantities.

Solid wood thicknesses and widths given are nominal. Actual thickness is 3/4 in. Actual widths are 1/2 in. less.

1-5/8"

2-1/2"

ARCHED SIDE RAIL
3/4" x 2-1/2" x 5-1/2"

SIDE STILE
3/4" x 1-1/2" x 59-1/4"

FRONT STILE
3/4" x 1-1/2" x 59-1/4"

2-1/2"

Sand all the plywood parts before assembly to avoid awkward inside-corner sanding later. Plywood usually requires only a light sanding with 150-grit paper. But watch for shallow dents or scratches that need a little extra sanding. And be careful not to sand through the micro-thin veneer along the edges.

Assemble the case

When you screw the sides to the shelves, use plywood spacers to eliminate measuring errors and out-of-square shelves (Photo 3). Before you cut the spacers, measure the thickness of the shelves. Although they're cut from 3/4-in. plywood, you'll probably find that they're actually a hair thinner than 3/4 in. To compensate, simply cut your spacers a bit longer (your 12-in. spacer may actually be 12-1/16 in. long, for example).

Inspect the sides before assembly and orient them so the best-looking veneer faces the outside of the case. Drill 3/32-in. pilot holes in the shelves using the side holes you drilled earlier as a guide. Also drill countersinks for the screw heads. "Pilot" bits that drill a pilot hole and countersink in one step cost about $5. Screw all the shelves to one side, then add the other side. Don't use glue. The screws alone are plenty strong, and any squeezed-out glue would prevent the plywood from absorbing stain later.

With all the shelves screwed into place, add the back. Measure the case from corner to corner in both directions; equal diagonal measurements means the case is square. Set the back in position and use a straightedge to mark the locations of the shelves. Fasten the back with screws rather than nails. That way, you can remove the back later to make finishing much easier.

Cut arched rails

Although straight rails would look good, the project shown here has arches cut in the top and bottom rails for a more elegant look. If you want curved rails, cut the top and bottom rails 28-5/8 in. long (you'll trim them to final length later). To mark the curves on the front arches, screw two blocks to a long scrap 35-7/8 in. apart. Bend a 36-in. metal straightedge between the blocks. Align the straightedge with the corners of the rail (Photo 4). To mark the side rails, use the bottom of a 5-gallon bucket (or any circle that's about 10 in. in diameter).

If you end up with a small hump or two, smooth them with sandpaper. For a perfect arc, use the cutout as a sanding block (Photo 5). Cut 80-grit sandpaper into 1-in.-wide strips

1 Crosscut the parts quickly and accurately using a stop block. The parts are too wide to cut in one pass, so flip the plank over after the first cut and make a second cut.

FIRST CUT

STOP BLOCK

2 Stack up the sides, mark the screw locations and drill through both sides at once. This cuts measuring and marking time, especially if you're building two bookcases.

3 Screw the sides to the shelves using plywood spacers to hold the shelves in precise position.

SIDE

SPACER

SHELF

4 Mark arches on the front rails using a simple arc jig made from wood scraps and a metal straightedge. Cut the arches with a jigsaw.

ARCH CUTOUT

5 Sand out bumps or waves in the arches using the cutout. Stick sandpaper to the cutout with spray adhesive.

6 Glue and nail the trim to the plywood case. Use as few nails as possible—just enough to hold the parts in place while the glue sets.

and apply a light coat of spray adhesive ($6) to their backs.

Next, cut the stiles to length, but don't cut the rails to length just yet. Before you attach any rails or stiles to the case, position the arched bottom rails on the case sides and use them to mark arcs. Cut these arcs with a jigsaw.

Add the trim and top

Fasten the rails and stiles following this sequence: Attach both of the side stiles along the front of the case. Align your nails with the shelves so they don't poke into the case. Then add one front stile. Set one front rail in place. Set the other front stile in place to check the length of the rail. If the length is right, cut the other rails to identical length. Attach the front rails and the second front stile. Don't worry if the rails and stiles aren't quite flush; you can sand them flush later. Next, add the side rails and the rear side stiles (Photo 6).

Two to four nails should be adequate for each part, although you may need more if the rail or stile is badly bowed. The glue will provide plenty of strength regardless of how many nails you use.

Allow the glue to set for an hour before you sand all the rails and stiles using a random orbital sander. Start with a 100-grit disc to sand flush uneven joints and remove any shallow scratches. Then switch to a 150-grit disc.

To attach the top, glue 3/4-in. plywood sleepers to the top shelf as shown in Figure A. Then predrill and screw the top in place. The top molding is simply 3/8-in.-thick strips cut from leftover scraps. Miter the corners and glue the strips in place, again using as few nails as possible.

Finish the bookcase

Unscrew the bookcase's back for easier finishing. The bookcases shown were finished with stain and three coats of polyurethane. With all the surfaces sanded to 150-grit, apply one coat of Minwax red oak stain. Shown is a satin sheen for the clear finish. But because three coats of satin can look like a cloudy sheet of plastic over the wood, begin with two coats of gloss, sanding lightly with a 320-grit sanding sponge between coats. Fill nail holes with color-matched wood putty after the first coat. After the second coat, add a coat of satin polyurethane. After setting the bookcases in place, drive one 2-1/2-in. screw through the back of each and into wall studs to prevent them from tipping forward.

Simple box shelves

Build a bunch for less than $100

Not only do these storage boxes look nice, but they're easy to build—just fasten together four sides and put on the back. Built from standard oak or birch plywood, these 12 x 12-in. boxes will cost about $35 for eight. If you use standard plywood, you'll have to patch voids in the edges with wood filler or cover the edges with edge banding (go to thefamilyhandyman.com and search for "edge banding"). To avoid that extra work, use Baltic birch plywood, which has better-looking, void-free edges. Baltic birch costs about $85 for a 3/4-in. x 60-in. x 60-in. sheet, which will give you five boxes. If your home center doesn't stock Baltic birch, look for it at a hardwood specialty store (check under "Hardwood Suppliers" in the yellow pages or search online to find a source). Use standard 1/4-in. plywood for the backs even if you use Baltic birch for the sides.

Time and tools

You can build a dozen or more boxes in a few hours. Spend Saturday assembling the boxes and applying the finish, then hang them or fasten them together on Sunday. To complete the project, you'll need a table saw to rip the plywood sheets and a circular saw to crosscut the top, back and sides. Read

Pretty or practical

The boxes work equally well in a formal setting and a utilitarian room, such as the laundry or garage. They offer an unlimited number of uses and arrangements.

Figure A Modular boxes

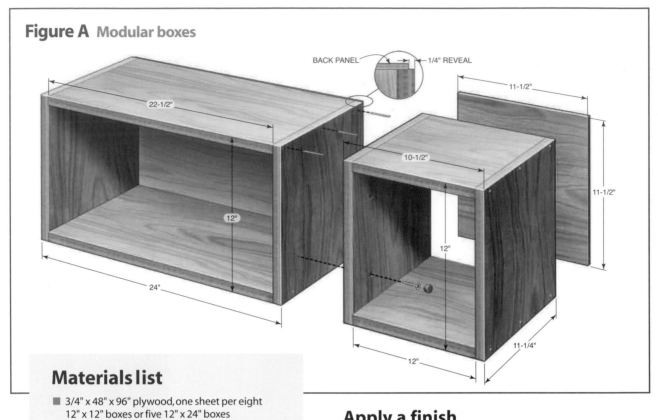

BACK PANEL — 1/4" REVEAL

22-1/2"

12"

24"

11-1/2"

10-1/2"

11-1/2"

12"

11-1/4"

12"

Materials list

- 3/4" x 48" x 96" plywood, one sheet per eight
  12" x 12" boxes or five 12" x 24" boxes
- 1/4" x 48" x 96" plywood, one sheet

on to learn how to make perfectly straight crosscuts using a guide. You'll also need a brad nailer to nail the boxes together.

Cut the pieces to size

Get started by ripping the 3/4-in. plywood sheets into 11-1/4-in.-wide strips on a table saw. Cut out any dents and dings along the edges. It's important that these pieces be exactly the same width so the boxes will be aligned when they're stacked together. Also rip the 1/4-in. plywood sheet into 11-1/2-in.-wide strips.

Crosscut the box tops, bottoms, sides and back panels to length following Figure A, above. Make the crosscuts with a circular saw and a guide (Photo 1).

Assemble the boxes

Placing adjacent sides in a carpenter's square ensures crisp 90-degree angles when you fasten the corners together. Set the square over wood blocks and clamp it to your work surface. Set one side and the top or bottom in the square, apply wood glue along the edge, and nail the corner together with 1-1/2-in. brad nails (Photo 2).

Fasten the remaining corners the same way. Leave the box in the carpenter's square to keep the corners square, then add the back panel (Photo 3). The back panels are 1/2 in. smaller than the overall box size to leave a 1/4-in. gap along each edge. This makes the edges less conspicuous when the boxes are installed.

Apply a finish

Once your boxes are fully assembled, it's time to apply a finish. Sand the boxes with 120-grit sandpaper to smooth out any rough spots, then wipe away the dust with a clean cloth.

If you want to paint the boxes, first prime them with a latex primer. Foam rollers work great for applying smooth coats of primer and paint. Brush on the primer in the corners, then roll the rest. Let the primer dry, lightly sand the boxes with 120-grit sandpaper, then apply the paint.

CROSSCUT GUIDE

1 Cut the box parts straight and square with a homemade crosscut guide. Stack two layers of plywood strips to cut perfectly matching parts fast.

2 Build perfectly square boxes by assembling them against a carpenter's square. Drive three nails per corner to hold them together until the glue dries.

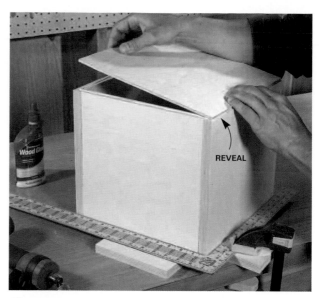

REVEAL

3 Center the back panel over the box, leaving a small gap along each side. Glue and nail the panel into place. The back panel keeps the box square.

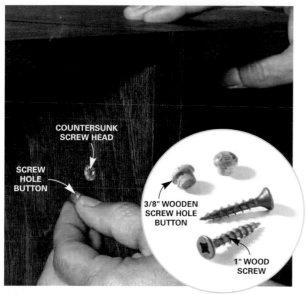

COUNTERSUNK SCREW HEAD

SCREW HOLE BUTTON

3/8" WOODEN SCREW HOLE BUTTON

1" WOOD SCREW

4 Drive two screws near the front. Hide screw heads with wooden "buttons" after screwing boxes together.

5 Arrange the boxes any way you like. Spaces between boxes can form compartments too.

For stained shelves, apply two coats of stain—Minwax Golden Oak followed by Minwax Ebony is shown here—and two coats of a water-based polyurethane.

Hang the boxes

Once the finish is dry, you can screw the boxes together or hang them on a wall. Be sure to hang the boxes with the side pieces overlapping the top and bottom, as shown in Figure A. This keeps the corner nails horizontal and makes the box stronger. Still, the boxes are not designed to hold a lot of weight. Countersinking the screw head and filling the hole with a 3/8-in. screw hole button hides the fastener. Screw hole buttons are available at home centers.

To fasten boxes together, first clamp them so they're perfectly flush. Then drill a 3/8-in.-diameter, 3/16-in.-deep countersink hole with a brad point drill bit ($3). The brad point won't tear or chip the veneer. Then drill 1/8-in. pilot holes in the countersink holes using a standard bit.

Drive a 1-in. wood screw into the pilot hole, countersinking the head. Dab paint or stain on the screw hole button and plug the hole (Photo 4).

To hang a box where there's a stud, drill two 1/8-in. pilot holes. Then spray paint the heads of 2-1/2-in. screws and drive them into the stud at the pilot holes (there's no alternative to leaving the heads exposed). If there's not a stud available, use self-drilling anchors, such as E-Z Ancors. Drill pilot holes through the box into the wall, remove the box and drive the anchors into the wall at the marks. Then fasten the box to the wall using the screws included with the anchors.

Also Available from Reader's Digest

101 Saturday Morning Projects

From the experts at *The Family Handyman*—the #1 home improvement magazine—here are more than 100 do-it-yourself projects ideal for every homeowner or apartment dweller. Each project can be completed in a half day or less.

ISBN 978-1-60652-018-5
$14.95 USA

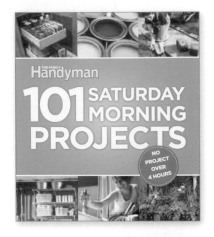

Home Repair without Despair

From the experts at *The Family Handyman,* here are hundreds of simple, smart, do-it-yourself home fixes, and projects that will save you thousands of dollars. If you can hold a hammer, then you can save a bundle.

ISBN 978-1-60652-135-9
$16.95 USA

For the Birds

Calling all backyard birders—here are 50 recipes sure to attract your feathered friends. You'll find tables on birdseed preferences, the best plants to attract birds, profiles on the most common feeder birds in North America, and tips to animal proof your feeder.

ISBN 978-1-60652-131-1
$9.95 USA

Reader's Digest books can be purchased through retail and online bookstores.
In the United States books are distributed by Penguin Group (USA), Inc.
For more information or to order books, call 1-800-788-6262.